Collected Poems: 1930 to 1965

BY THE SAME AUTHOR

The True Confession of George Barker
A Vision of Beasts and Gods
News of the World
Eros in Dogma
Calamiterror

Collected Poems

1930 to 1965

GEORGE BARKER

October House Inc. New York

Published by October House Inc.
55 West 13th Street, New York

Library of Congress catalogue card number 64–23113
Printed by Clarke & Way, Inc. New York, U.S.A.
First Edition

Inscribed to the memory of

Marion Frances Taaffe Barker

1881–1955

Introduction

'And what,' said the Emperor, 'does this poem describe?'
　'It describes,' said the Poet, 'the Cave of the Never-Never.
'Would you like to see what's inside?' He offered his arm.
　They stepped into the poem and disappeared for ever.

Contents

I

I

Daedalus

I.

Like the enormous liner of his limbs
and fell.
Remain behind, look on
What's left of what was once in blighted remains.
That imponderable body
Smote my desire, now smitten
Mortally.
I lift his head, his death dampens
The moist palm of my hand like handled fear
Like fear cramping my hand
and stand.
Remain behind, entertain posthumous fear.

II.

Come where no crowds can trouble us divert us
No acrobats hawkers bottles or street musicians
No towering necks like buildings overlook
Intimate revelation.

I take your hand
Spectre
And steadily lead you
Across morning haunted lawns in earlier
Days, and show
With a reversal of our growing older
How it began, what caused, the germ of time.

Where florid in the night pregnant nightdresses
Proceed sedately down unlighted stairs
Like people. And in the garden
Large lakes unreal. Hark, I hear visitant
Swans, and the moths in the trees
Like minor caverns humming. There he draws
Antennae from paralysed spiders, weapons
In his warlock fingers brandished: or runs

Engendering the eventual major strength like engines
Preparant. I cannot discern you in the leaves or in the
Undergrowth, when starting down the steep hills
He flies precipitate: Spectre, Spectre, where
If among these early places lie you, do you lie?

He fell, not then. Recently sure has fallen from that
  high
Platform. Formed in fearlessness, has fallen
Like through thought's clouds through fear, as You
  stood
Waiting with wanting breast to catch, he in his fall
Evaded. Passed towards a grave straight through.
Of Course You Knew, for saw his comet face
Approaching downward like irresistible.
I mourn him. Him I mourn, from morn to morning.

III.

Where once he trod
    I cannot tread;
From the home he is gone from
    I am prohibited:
We cannot be
    While he is gone from being;
While he is not with being
    I am as well miserably unliving;
Totally bereft I too am totally absent,
    Appearing here, although
Bruisable and buriable seeming, am too bruised
    In my dead
    Too buried.
    Spectre who spreads
Internal dissension,
    Dividing the unit army of the body
To coward forces,
    Since I have brought
    To these private places
Sick with his not being, with his recalled
Reverberant fleet blooms of doing and coming,

Empty with his going, since accompanied, entertained,
Shown choicest hothouse blossoms, phenomenal
Plants he acted on to the air like dances lasting,
Since he is not here but where you know with doom—

IV.

Where wander those once known herons
        Or rabbits here
With shattered entrapped forepaws pitiable in crimson
        Killing have known,
And seven-year-old boys locked among ominous
        Shadows, enveloped
        Have known, and see
As the unmerciful onrush of determined seas
        Gathers small craft
There the acquainted faces of the dead sailors
        Sight that sees
Where those once known herons fled in fear, to where I
        Like lonely herons
        The abandoned heroine

V.

Go. With mild gradual descent
Burden the memory
Not as he fell, in anger, in the combat
With forms invisible intactual fought
On that mortal rooftop: not with celestial
Speed brought down, in meritorious
Defeat no beating, but like lamed
Herons or birds in wounded slope
Descending down to lamentable homes
In scraggy graves, borne down by death, I come
Drawn down to earth, and underneath
The earth, like one drawn under
Lethal water by an unknown weight
Unseen invisible, but not unknown is fear.

Luctus in Morte Infantis

Count them as they cluster
Like young frond around
That passing throne a cloud
Embellishing their master!

Thousand on thousand, charming
The upward birds, that ascend
To take the recent hand
In support in first performing.

O that adept evader
Of the bubble or bomb
Who from the immediate womb
Leaped cloudward, to border

The budded throne! He, though scarce
Earth breathing once
Intuitively analysed the air
Contagious of fatal and sour

Ill, so sprang
Immaculate with his spring
Upon the skies' steps
Laughing with his leaps.

His radiant flesh is
Interchangeable
With his spirit's iridescence;
Which up flies we cannot tell

Distinguishing only the flash
Of that ascendant flame,
For barely his spirit flesh
In being became.

O in summer he came with roses
And with them rose

Over the rose trees, and over
The mountains and the roseate clouds, never

With next summer or after
To visit with them, and laughter,
The gardens, nor to know
From whom he was called to go.

The Crystal

With burning fervour
I am forever
Turning in my hand
The crystal, this moment

Whose spatial glitter
Travelling erratically
Forward

Touches with permanent
Disturbance the pavements
The faked walls the crevices
Of futurity.

Sooner than darken
This crystal miracle
With a hand's
Vagary

One would dissever
This wrist this hand,
Or remove the eyelid
To see the end.

Venerable all Hills all Valleys

Venerable all hills, all valleys
Avalanched with immaculate quietude, air
Falls through autumnal halls, in which infrequent airs
Blown from the few instrumental leaves
Fall again in infrequent falls, in rains.

Again formidable winter strikes the winds
Crystalline immobile, all still.
Walking abroad, each one observes the sight
Of his confederate transfixing distance,
His eye's flight fixed in icy course.

Against the interminable grieving of the sea
I raise my voice, silence the miserable
Breakers, while upon my inward winter break
Incipient gaities of the impending spring, sending
Messengers in the budding of these lines,
Defeating the sea's insurgent funereal roll
With a tongue's sunbeam, with a hand's summer rondure.

Narcissus

My tired lips received that morning
Their first kiss, so stirred the mind
Cannot subside for days for weeks or months.
That slim mouth upon mine held firm complete pressure,
Keeping mine for the inconceivable period
Between meeting in dream and meeting the unknown person.

Therefore for days or months I examined all faces
That slip between me and the exit to forget;
At political meetings at parties and at festivals
Every unrecognizing face, the features of every unrecognized face,
refused

To be that face, assumed adverse reaction,
Closed its cold eyes on the air, and was removed.

Travelling through a fine evening in a car
The attentive line of my own face was at intervals caught
From the sunlight in outline—the chin's framed curve,
Lips, jaw's asseveration—on the windscreen;
The reproduction on, the reality through
I now no longer wander wondering who.

The Leaping Laughers

When will men again
Lift irresistible fists
Not bend from ends
But each man lift men
Nearer again.

Many men mean
Well: but tall walls
Impede, their hands bleed and
They fall, their seed the
Seed of the fallen.

See here the fallen
Stooping over stones, over their
Own bones: but all
Stooping doom beaten.

Whom the noonday washes
Whole, whom the heavens compel,
And to whom pass immaculate messages,
When will men again
Lift irresistible fists
Impede impediments
Leap mountains laugh at walls?

The Seal Boy

See he slips like insinuations
Into the waves and sidles
Across breakers, diving under
The greater tidals,

Plunging, a small plane
Down dark altitudes,
Trailing bubbles like aerial bombs
Or a balloon's broods.

O moving ecstatic boy
Sliding through the gloomy seas
Who bring me pearls to enjoy
Rarer than to be found in these seas—

Between the fixed bars of your lips
Darts the kiss like silver
Fish, and in my wild grip
You harbour, for ever.

He comes among

He comes among
The summer throngs of the young
Rose, and in his long
Hands flowers, fingers, carries;
Dreamed of like aviaries
In which many phoenices sing,
Promising touch soon
In summer, never to come:

Or, the scarce falls
Of unearthly streams, calls
And recalls the call,

Tempting in echoes the aspatial
Glooms of the empty
Heart, till the senses, need inebriate,
Turning and burning through slow leaves of vague
Urge, shall, until age.

I am that face about which fire fell

I am that face about which fire fell.
Nor can the years, though clouds, wholly hide
The solar glow enthroning the brow on a crowd.
These eyeballs, curving swiftly over space
Fell from that space across which curve the stars
Through spreading rings. Are folded beneath wings
At whose slow lift of morning I am lifted
Into the brilliant being, coloured airs.
The hand begs action from barren air, flighting
In employment and enjoyment like sails on seas
Regular of change. Entrusted but dangerously
To this pale paraphernalia of bone,
The soul, dangled like veils in slow gales,
Strives for its flight, so fanning the solar crown,
Darkening and dazzling my point of the stars,
Wafting the hand
To ardours of achievement burning steadier than fire, or
The burning and eternal stars.

Summer Idyll

Sometimes in summer months, the matrix earth
Loaded to gold, the boughs arching downward
Burdened, the shallow and glucose streams
Teeming, flowers out, all gold camouflage
Of the collusive summer: but under the streams
Winter lies coldly, and coldly embedded in

The corn hunger lies germinally, want under
The abundance, poverty pulling down
The tautened boughs, and need is the seed.

Robe them in superb summer, at angles
Their bones penetrate, or with a principality
Of Spring possess them; under the breast
Space of a vacancy spreads like a foul
Ghost flower, want; and the pressure upon
The eyeballs of their spirits, upon the organs
Of their spare bodies, the pressure upon
Their movement and their merriment, loving and
Living, the pressure upon their lives like deep
Seas, becomes insufferable, but is suffered.

Sometimes the summer lessens a moment the pressure.
Large as the summer rose some rise
Bathing in rivers or at evening harrying rabbits,
Indulging in games in meadows—and some are idle, strewn
Over the parks like soiled paper like summer
Insects, bathed in sweat or at evening harried
By watchmen, park-keepers, policemen—indulge in games
Dreaming as I dream of rest and cleanliness and cash.

And the gardens exhibit the regalia of the season
Like debutante queans, between which they wander
Blown with vague odours, seduced by the pure
Beauty, like drowned men floating in bright coral.
Summer, denuding young women, also denudes
Them, removes jackets, exposing the bony moral—
Summer moves many up the river in boats

Trailing their fingers in the shadowed water; they
Too move by the river, and in the water shadows
Trail a hand, which need not find a bank,
Face downwards like bad fruit. Cathedrals and Building
Societies, as they appear, disappear; and Beethoven
Is played more loudly to deafen the Welsh echoes,
And Summer, blowing over the Mediterranean
Like swans, like perfect swans.

It is the sorrow season

It is the sorrow season
The dove sits perplexed:
It is the springing primrose
Brings in the sorrow season.

The myrtle its green tears
Evolves in the sorrow season.
The border of the urban garden
Decorates itself with blood.

Against the antipodal rocks
Rises the sorrow season.
The equinoxes of despair
Occur in a dark sequence.

The engine of experience
Accelerates its own disease,
Horror, like a sixth sense,
Explodes in the light of reason.

The sorrow season is machine.
Lolling daffodil and bird
The tongue of fire and the quick stream
Function in the sad machine.

I, mute immutable, cry

I, mute immutable, cry
To music's beauty, lend
To this unable hand
That matchless faculty.

Bright instrument of the hand
Leaning downward from more splendid

Spheres, than this darker land
Darker, that it is ended,

Then blended in that voicing
Of the higher unheard choirs,
I hear my mute spirit rejoicing
And my hand inspires.

Verses for a Nursery Wall

The cat and the mouse
Fear the rat and fear
The man with the hat
And the house and spear,

Ladies in bright bedrooms
  Spread with glassware
  Dread the stare
  Which cannot but pass
Through twentyfive rooms
And redden the womb
And with a dark laugh
  Shatter the glassware—

Cats and ladies, wombs and glasses
Hide behind something when a man passes;
  When a man passes
  Twentyfive
  Before a man passes
  Twentyfive
Count the amount of you left alive
Be as busy as bees in a b beehive
Hide behind me the young man cried.

Kew Gardens

Two who were walking together beneath European thunder,
Recalling their adolescent days of experiments in bliss,
Wandering arm in arm under stars of political crisis
Like catherine-wheels in the sky, whispered of sweet summers,
As Fate swung an armament bludgeon over their kiss.

Like flies on a table they traversed the dangerous plains,
Small figures dwarfed in the theatre of death and shadow,
Hopping along oblivious of imminent war or murder,
Nibbling at the moon reflected in the Danube like a stain:
They wandered here and there discussing their sweet summers.

Then France at their feet fell through and they foundered,
Till they caught at the Pyrenees like rocks in porridge
And found substantial ground where the cock of courage
Sang like a harp in the Spanish tree as it smouldered
Among the ruins of Guernica that candle at a cortège.

Struck at them from the sky as the Berlin Eagle
Explored with lines of fire the environs of Russia,
Fire and fury. With their hair on fire like fuchsia
Fled to the Swiss lakes and dipped their faces
In Peace like water, but were nearly drowned.

Portugal poisoned them as they sat taking food,
Ataturk sent affable assassins to take blood;
Abyssinia sent begging ambassadors to solicit
Assistance, but too soon the dove shot down by Macchis,
Too late the dove reached the Emperor Selassie.

Thus hounded from city to city like a circus of two
Resting their elbows on volcanoes or their feet in blood,
Subsisting on mutual love, harried by Gestapo,
This tiny two went on exhausted through red flood,
Through violence and ruin, until finally they fell down in Kew.

And among the bluebells, the birds, the pagodas, the paths,
They lay a long while resting from Europe's wrath,
While their wounds went white and were lost among the daisies.
Then whispering together like mice of love and summer
They lay and kissed against the wall of Europe's thunder.

Calamiterror

Dedication to Albert Gordon Barker

The April horror grows over my September.
I see my hand glittering with blood and tears
Hanging at the bend of my arm like a leech member,
Fatal, inspired to violence, sowing scars;
Elevating itself in the anaconda stance
Evolving devastation. I see my hand
Passing over the palace of his face,
Leaves it pale, bloody gap, blinded, blanched;
Leaving a wake of pain and leaving a loss
Not to be rehabilitated by
The perfect prize, the penny, or the cause,
The blue tulip, the forget-me-not, or the sky.
Therefore I render to my hell hand's Abel
The no less agonized blood my hand has bled.

1936

INTRODUCTORY STANZAS TO BOOK I

1.
The gay paraders of the esplanade,
The diamond harlequins, the acrobats,
The gloriously lost in summer glades,
The wanderers through the acropolis,
The ones who seek the times' shade

Reclining by catastrophes,
The figures of the downward grade:
The gay shadows of the shade.

2.
The continental operas, the play
Featuring beautiful beasts and the beast beauty,
The shimmering mannequins of Love's display
Meandering through, glamorous and nude,
Loose at the hip; those whom they displease,
The glancers at the gay boy's beauty;
The mirror-gazer self-betrayed;
Loving shadows in the shade.

3.
The falling cliff that like a melting face
Collapsing through its features, leaves a stare,
The grinning cat; the cataracts that grace
The private gardens like water-scarves; where
The National Trust exhibits its own views;
The shadowing perspectives of Kensington avenues
Sunday in January, when the spires fade;
Outlining the geography of shade.

4.
The fourth dimension of this space is fear.
The predecessor's omnipresent leer
Between the church-arch, the descending hand
Frightful like five bananas on the shoulder;
The three figures that for ever stand
Beside, before, behind; as we grow older
Achieving mass as we become the shade.
Metamorphosis of shade to shade.

5.
Down what escarpments can the man escape
Consigned to profounds of his mind's abysms?
None till his spirit like the thermometer climbs
Out of his own abdominal abysms.
The phœnix snake from former skin

Leaves in ashes his self dead:
The one always remaining in
Self's skin, remains a shade.

6.
The mask of self though more than marvellous,
Glancing through ovals lovelier than Hylas' eyes,
Speaking with the tongues of the girls on the isles,
Languishing lips, coloured and loose
Like fruit, suspended and melodious:
The countenance of vacancy,
The cardboard opera facade,
The empty stare that dare not see,
The speech of shade.

7.
The hand that lifts the intimating rose
With infinitesimal machinery is
The instrument that digs and dies and buries
Itself and self; from whence arose
The hand that elevates another,
Whose area like a world displayed
Supports the face like a feather;
The face is in the shade.

8.
Through apertures in his own tomb
The one who won against his shade
Contemplates the successors for whom
Out of his hand the world was made.
Tendrils of his arms break out,
The apertures become his eyes,
His speech by others' acts is said:
He is a man in the shade.

I.

1.
What when born upward breaking from heaven downward
It is my bare bloodred babe, with beauty
Branching from armpit, maypole at thigh, world flying

Like fairboats around, the axis of existence.
The bud beginning, the burning salamander
Suspended in his breast, the shambles in the bowels,
The tall tree spine supporting vertical
The crucified to life bare body blood.

2.
The eye-shaped leaf, the topmost of the tree,
Examines heaven, the leaf-shaped eye examines
The eye-shaped leaf, and each observes in each
Heaven and heaven. I have observed the leaf
Flying like bird over mountains carrying in its curve
The brainstruck eyeball. Whither I cry
And the tongue leaf lifts its tongue,
Somewhere O somewhere where the summer month
Builds a green body of leaf about the bone.

3.
Where are the abandoned abandoned or the buried buried,
As the born are born here and the consigned consigned?
It is here the terror-struck fall and the fallen decay,
It is here the hooded vulture and the walking skeleton
Converse in fatal language, rend each other, blend together.
Here on the lunar rocks the female vulture seizes
The skeleton of love, and the rocking of their interlock
Confuses categories, convulses shape, rocks the rocks.

4.
Spreadeagled like the full length mirror,
Pinioned like brilliant butterfly,
Fixed through gold axle on the Ixion sky,
The babe blazes in vacuum of being's horror
The shapes of sense, the jerking thigh,
The eye dividing, the hand and hand,
This is the limbo circus of the human,
The man, the idol one, the illustrious I.

5.
Time is dark, and in the centre burns
The babe with salamander in his breast;

The salamander is species of the sun,
Whose clouds are horror, fear, and decay.
The babe is universe with hands and feet of stars,
His blood is gravitation running red;
His eyes are the leaf of the tree and also heaven.
The waterspout is his umbilical.

6.
Under his lid the stalactite tear forms,
Pointing to sorrow wherever his eyeball veers;
Chrysanthemums blossom from his bowels
It is love flowering, and the lark nests
In the socket of his eye, between his loins
The phœnix flames, the tree leans from his arm.
What is it wafts the tree with folding winds,
Fans up the terrible phœnix, flights the bird,
Elaborates the great chrysanthemum,
Sharpens the icicle tear. They cannot answer.

7.
What is the green dream in the summer tree,
Which like a vague womb rests on the dark boughs;
What figures are like embryos coiled in trees
Mimicking the idiom of the bird? What word
By the bird spoken speaks openly of mystery?
How can the stream translate from water tongue
Speaking of origin beyond source? From what course
Falls the incredible comet: what cause
Flings the star babe after the flying star?

8.
Who is the parent of the innumerable plant,
The gladiola, the hidden violet, the sweet onion;
From whence wanders the extempore watercourse
Describing the geometry of love;
Or from whose appalling paroxysm of love
The lightning shoots impregnant with death:
Are the always changing clouds the features
The gold eyeball eyeball, of the unknown face?

9.
The blood cataract leaping along the arm
Boiling with foam of perspiration pearls
Bursts from the fingers, rains upward to heaven.
Thus as the rain returns to earth returns
Blood god blood to god. No secret move
Disturbing blood but to god transfuses.
Wherever he lies in what removed ward
The kiss of acts registers red on his lips

10.
Sin is not to act, for the bird waltzes,
The elder ripens, the leaf declines and dies.
The dead bird cannot dance, the dead tree remains
Perpetually the misty November morning
When the last tremor unhooked the last three leaves.
Thus the sin man hangs in a vacuum,
Suspended like a world between pull of opposed forces,
The downward demon pull, the upward angel.

II.

1.
What when born upward breaking from heaven downward,
It is my babe in the bosom murmuring who.
Who is the parent of the innumerable plant,
It is the dream in the green tree murmuring who.
Why walk at night admiring the moonlight mountain,
Looking for the long lost upward, the dream descending,
The unending line, the flying pig, the vision
Rising from landslides, the kiss, the key, the clue?

2.
Where in what rear of space behind the face
Grows the green tree, the bud begins, the dwindling phœnix
Revives in summer, and the stars on perches trill?
Hence wanders the extempore watercourse falling
From the blue eye of space like a continual tear.
It is here the abandoned and the buried return,
As the born are born here, and the babe reborn.

3.
The green dream in the summer tree is death,
And birds in boughs are embryos of life,
Dancing and singing among the summer horror.
So the mad boy runs along the lip of the grave
Pursuing the animal of life, which turns and leaps
Sighing into the grave—down the mad boy pitches.
The green dream in the summer field is death,
The gold growth in the summer field is life.

4.
Between the ribs of the violent man
Beats the red centre of the world of death.
The ribs like branches hanging meat like leaves
Makes the green tree red. Coiled in the ribs
The embryos of life and death lie, one by one
Ravaging a surgeon's groove of agony,
Break from the belly, stand on the bloody thigh,
Cockcrowing like man and babe and bird.

5.
Thus is born downward breaking from bud upward
The bare bloodred babe, the crimson cockerel.
Crowned with the plumes of blood, the fear feathers,
The fragments of his mother's meat hanging horror,
Agony, agony, bowls and blood, the trumpet screaming,
The flags of flesh waving, the arch of pain,
The manikin marches down the thigh,
Trampling a bowels' shambles in his rear.

6.
The green dream hung in the male tree is womb.
I saw the summer penis with the green dream
Hung like a gasmask terrible green and fatal.
The engine of the living is the bone,
So from the blood and bone the blood and bone ascend.
Then the heavenly curvetting through heaven,
The bird the butterfly the aeronaut,
The final bone falls like the Indian boy.

7.
Like the bird in tree the bloody embryo
Leaps upward, and moves over space and time,
Seeking a place and time he does not know,
Driven forward by the boiling blood, the yearning bone.
The swallow at his wrist leads on, the lodestone tear
Pointing to sorrow wherever his eyeball veers,
Knows the location of his destination.
The salamander in his breast is Sun.

8.
The phœnix at his loins prepares its ashes,
The gasmask womb hanging at his thigh
Transforms the phœnix ashes into tears,
The tear leaps to the ground as child.
The giant embryo ploughs through horror onward.
Shedding a wake of flowers and gods and falling towers,
Broods of the bleeding cockerel, transfixed corpses,
Cities in growth or ruin, music.

9.
Music, and cities in growth or ruin,
Transfixed corpses, broods of the bleeding cockerel,
Falling towers, gods, and flowers decorate
The Euclidean furrow he drives towards doom.
So the red fissure of the splitting belly
Follows him like a lengthening wound;
The opening aperture of birth, increasing,
Reveals again the dark womb as grave.

10.
Through paradise the parabola
Of the militant man ascends,
Passing through orange boughs and love,
Through carnage of his conscience,
Between the sweeting lunar hills
And the bleeding lunar valley, through
The wreckage of his perfection,
Burdened with the ball of world.

11.
The bird the butterfly the aeronaut
Trapeze the sky in diagrams of colour,
The trajectory of the militant man
Trails like a carnival comet gold and blood.
Through the September tree the wild
Runaway rainbow of his curve unfolds;
And at my feet falls the burnt out fragment,
The finger or the face sheered off clean.

12.
The weeping shell propelled from war
Drops in a chaos of life and death.
The leaping babe expelled from womb,
Dividing the chaos of paradise,
Ends up in a death dark room.
The penis shooting metal death
Explodes the womb of the life room:
The penis shooting mental life
Wastes its shells against the tomb.

13.
The Shropshire lark and the Wyoming whippoorwill
Musical in the leaves of the September tree,
Fall with eyes blinded and with feathers seared,
While the hurtling figure of the man
Crashing the painted boughs of paradise, grazing
His frightful eyeballs on mountains, drops
Like the lead diver in the amazing sea,
Through the perspectives of the physical.

14.
The blood boils and the bone yearns.
The pressure of the body upon
The spirit, the pressure upon the body
Of the Pacific mental, the vague sea,
Through the aching physical and spiritual
The bone yearns and the blood burns;
Yearning towards the liquid blood,
Burning to be the easy air.

15.
This is that hank of hair and raw bone
That frequently in remote places
The cottagers find caught in trees.
This is the weasel suspended from bush branch,
The adder glistening in the noose of string
Seen in the Worcester lane; the head of eel
Blocking the water system. Thus god's engine
Ejects its refuse.

16.
Catastrophe occurs but the corpse
Normally achieves its destination.
Ninety of the hundred ones now flying
Over the hills will not encounter disaster.
The wretched fragments found by boys on shores,
Even the Shropshire lark or the Wyoming whippoorwill,
Indicate only that excessive velocity
The desperate man indulges, going home.

III.

1.
The boy bud springing from the maternal tree
Still senses the original blood, the bud or deer
Drinks from the red jet of the female thigh.
The doped colt on the Caliente course
Running amok is the blood baited boy.
I see him in the centre of destruction,
The screaming cat, the tin can dog,
The frog dissected, the one-eyed calf,
The thrush in vice.

2.
The odour of the puerperal gush
Mellows the faded daffodil;
The maddened tin can dog
Stretches at the navel string;
The apples stolen from the bough
Emasculate the erect tree;

The paroxysms of the birth
The violated girl avenge.

3.
O long lost upward in the dream descending,
The flying pig and the school-tie anaconda!
I hear the windowed whispering of women
Like birds at bars, the ballerina battalions of
Gulls balancing on waves when
The evening sea breaks, and a mole gnawing,
—I hear the ceaseless meshing of his jaws—
Tunnelling up the abdominal tube.

4.
The bleeding cockerel tethered to the tree
At the fourteenth fall achieves metamorphosis.
The green life like a tear falls about him
Building a body of leaf about the bone.
The tear of leaf and the terror of the blood
Mix to the elixir of gold, behold the phœnix.
Rising like life from the crux of destruction
The screaming cat the agony thrush make man.

5.
The minor carnage of the Caliente boy,
The birds crushed and the violated girls,
The animals screaming and the raped tree,
The absurd chaos of actual destruction,
This is the clash of wreckage whence the man arises.
The birth string breaks, the cockerel screams
Ascending towards the long lost upward dream.

IV.

1.
My summer zephyr idling through my fingers
Load up my flower with plenitude of sorrow,
The pollen that like pain produces pearls
Makes fall the word from a hand.
My summer zephyr bring me the note of love,

The blonde girl singing in the gardens, bring
The evening vivid with mythologies, and render me,
O summer zephyr, the nightingale's bough.

2.
My autumn odour of the nine month horror,
The slowing blood, the growing chrysanthemum,
Electrify the tepid heart and charge the mind
With the starved figures of obligation.
Distort my bowels so the futile hand
Finds there no flower festoons but feels
The thinning elongated guts of fact,
The Derbyshire starvation, the Welsh hell.

3.
My April point of the appearing world
Sting like a crocus finger at the eye,
This is the mad March boy of the year,
Who ties the primrose on the waterpipe,
Suspends the tinsel spangle, runs around
Exhibiting himself in store windows.
My April boy, O burgeon me now
With the word fruit of my arm's bough.

4.
My Mary May maternal with the summer,
Proceed in strawberry and lavender;
Move like a colour along the fringe of gardens
Brushing and breathing love. My May Mary
Sidling along the sunlight pavements softly,
The garb of leaf and tree cannot conceal
That summer magnificent bigness. It is my season
That bearing summer you bear me the sun.

5.
My winter women of margarine and tears,
Shivering with sorrow in the corner, I come
Who has crouched with you warming at your breasts.
My winter women more maternal than summer,
I was your boy kept warm in your sorrow corner;

It was from you I learned that love
Draws the lost and the lonely towards the warmth,
And feeds them from the fountain breast.

6.
My winter women of Wandsworth and Walsingham,
The fatal queue waiting at the minehead,
Inhabit my word and render it deep and terrible.
Here I go down descending my mine of man
Searching for something, probing for the soul.
O winter women, expert in lamenting,
Instruct my speech in the accent of despair—
When I descend, I shall find nothing there.

7.
My million loss and my martyrdom,
The gladiola the sweet onion in my fingers,
The ornamental bird with ribbon overhead,
The regalia of the Rex Whistler I suffer.
I tear my guts out on the platform
Or rummage in my stomach with bloody hands
To catch the mole or bird that gnaws or sings
Infrequently as the solstice miracle.

8.
My martin swallow, enter the November,
The sorrow season of my year.
Violate the numb atmosphere
With aerial ballets of ecstasy.
My interminable mole of soul,
Break through the abdominal skin,
And like the kangaroo I caress
The second me I keep within.

9.
My dark abdominal mine
I enter leaping down the lungs,
Here on the hell heart I find
The voluptuous flamingo undulating and
Coiling in its female neck

The stringent flame the salamander.
My masculine salamander consume
The feminine flamingo of desire.

10.
My swallow martin and my psychic mole
I search for in the bowels' caves and thunder.
I hear the faint swallow's cry above from below,
And when I am high I hear it low.
Somewhere it perches on the spinal tree
Flapping the tinsel wings I cannot see.
My psychic mole, gnawing at the root,
Endeavours to dislodge the fruit.

11.
My subterranean canals of love Venetian
Flowing like fire along vein and vein,
My lovely gondolas of love follow
Floating like grapes, I see them at my wrist.
But where are the birds, the Mark pigeons,
I feel them infrequently rustle in my breast,
I gather grapes for them: O my bosom birds,
Violate me with your violence!

12.
My swallow salamander, rise and burn,
Render me martyr in my breast's flame,
Immolate me upon my own desire,
Consume me in the fire of your fact.
O salamander swallow mole,
Divide me with the splits of birth,
Gnaw through the abdominal wall, and spring
Like the blood babe at my feet.

V.

1.
I wondered once why the Wyoming whippoorwill
The Shropshire lark and the glittering Oxford tree,
Sometimes should jangle boughs and execute music
By the Babylonian stream I mean Ealing.

I see the flamingo involved with the hanging fruits,
The hand of horror the claw of bananas and
Mr. Salisbury the proprietor greengrocer,
The magnificently actual unit the human.

2.

Return, return, O long lost in Babylon, return.
I now wonder why the Wyoming whippoorwill
The Shropshire lark, the glittering Oxford tree,
Jangle boughs no more and no more execute music
Near me or for me or to me. No, not in the Dorset
Remove, the always deciduous the propitious of song,
The autumnal and always bright with bird place.
No Shropshire lark, or Wyoming whippoorwill.

3.

I recall Ealing Common alive like July with
The exultant tumultuous lark and weeping whippoorwill,
Among which I wander holding the Oxford tree
Like toy in hand, and women in my bowels.
I recall the advent of my right hand
Fluttering with olive branch like dove,
I recall that the Shorpshire lark alighted
Like love on my lips, and went within.

4.

Where O Wyoming whippoorwill where
Search for or seek for if long lost!
I hear my voice rising, can you hear,
Return, Wyoming, to my tongue!
I recall the clustering whippoorwill
Dropping sorrow in my ear,
Dropping sorrow in my ear.

5.

Then the figure of Milton frequented my bedroom.
I remember the disturbance in the ivy leaves outside the
window.
The large envelope arrived from Italy containing a letter
Referring to suicide in the Bay of Naples.

I celebrate the first Sunday of Septuagesima
Reclining in Richmond Park watching the deer.
The Italian lady observes from the door of the bedroom,
'It is cold but quiet in here.'

6.
The chaos of experience is kaleidoscope,
Whose rotation is the disappearing year,
I grow month older, vague design takes shape,
The Italian lady conforms to temptation,
The shade of Milton instructs me in ambition,
The letter from Italy is always arriving
Suggesting suicide in the Tyrrhenian,
The fall from it all, secession, sleep.

7.
But until I hear the whippoorwill lark sing again,
Or the dove revisits my right hand, and the tree
Springs like a branch from my finger, I continue.
Inclining my ear to my bosom of evenings,
Listening like water diviner for words,
Wondering why the heart's decay
Makes me no pearls, no lovely bubbles,
What have I done that takes my birds away.

8.
Sometimes of summer months they seem to reappear,
Brilliantly, for a moment, intermittent, fitful,
Flicker a branch of music over my eye,
Tantalizing, divine, ephemeral, immediately gone.
Leaving the whisp of a feather, tinted with tongue,
Lying like an epitaph in the curve of my hand.
It is the paradise crumb they come for,
The soul like a feather glittering in the hand.

VI.

1.
Meandering abroad in the Lincolnshire meadows day
Day and day a month perhaps, lying at night lonely,
The early September evening administering a mystery,

The moon executing its wavering sleight of hand, I sense the
Advent of the extraordinary event, the calamiterror,
Turn and encounter the mountain descending upon me—
The moment of terror flashes like dead powder
Revealing the features of the mass as mine.

2.
Time like a mountain made of my own shadow
Collapsing on me, buries me in my life.
It is the future, undermined by present,
Falling appallingly backward. I bring
The cracked escarpments hurling down, I catch
The agonized glint of years in a fall of
Rubble, the time clatters down with branches
I hear a broken life scream and sob like me.

3.
Meandering abroad in the Lincolnshire meadows
Throw up no mountain featured with self's face.
Idling like Hylas beside the Babylonian stream
Admire the harp on the willow not the bright mask
Suspended through the depths or down
Internally and eternally drowned you go. I know.
I wandered at night admiring the moonlight mountain
The moon had made a monster of my own.

4.
I see the elements of my growth were drawn
Not from the objects that encourage growth,
The mountain ornamented with morning tears,
The musical tree, the hesitating river,
But the distorted mountain of the bowels,
The hysterical tree that branches to the arms,
The lunar river from the sexual fountain.
Feeding on self, the internal cannibal
Stands like a gap over its swallowed self.

5.
About the adult like the solar system
Objects revolve, holding the man in place.

The abdomen of youth is the balloon world
Twisted to fit between the ribs. The Spartan boy
Had his own fox-globe hidden at his belly.
The youth of sorrow mourns this indigestion,
The world swelling in his guts. I vomit.
This is the act that I now execute.

6.
Why walk at night admiring the moonlight mountain,
It is to find and feel the real and fine.
More may the glittering angle indicate
The physiognomy of the divine than mine.
Who is the parent of the innumerable plant,
It is not the sweet onion hanging at my loin.
The green tree springing in the rear of space
Follows the Greek sun and not my face.

7.
I recall how the rosetree sprang out of my breast.
I recall the myriads of birds in the cage of my head,
I recall my third finger the branch of myrtle,
I recall the imprisoned women wailing in my bowels.
I was the figure of the Surrealist Exhibition
With a mass of roses face. I hung like hawk
Hungry over the running world, I hung
Like sun that pulls the bright boys, like the spider.

8.
I saw the moon nightly performing a circle about
The pivotal point of my eye. The bird flew
Either towards or from me, sang to me or was
Silent. I sensed the violent spinning of things,—
I was their axle like the polar tree.
The key of kings had fallen from the blue
Into my keyhole eye, I knew I knew.
I felt the crush of hell in my left side.

9.
It was on Sunday the 12th April I saw
The figure of William Blake bright and huge

Hung over the Thames at Sonning. I had not had this.
Familiar with the spatial mathematic,
Acknowledging the element of matter,
I was acquainted with the make of things,
But not this. I had not acknowledged this.
I had not encountered prototype.

10.
I saw William Blake large and bright like ambition,
Absolute, glittering, actual and gold.
I saw he had worlds and worlds in his abdomen,
And his bosom innumerably enpeopled with all birds.
I saw his soul like a cinema in each of his eyes,
And Swedenborg labouring like a dream in his stomach.
I remember the myrtle sprouting from his hand
And saw myself the minor bird on the bough.

11.
I recognized the cosmology of objects,
The contributing and constituting things,
Which contemplated too close make a chaos,
The glorious plethora, the paradise mass, the chaos of
Glory, in which the idiot wanders collecting.
I recognized the cosmology of chaos,
Observing that the condition rendering
Chaos cosmos is the external fact.

12.
William Blake was larger than my Lincolnshire mountain
When like my mountain fell. I heard the catastrophic
Fragments of his torso breaking past me, it was
The object of the physical world breaking on me
Like Krakatoa like Krakatoa like the
Fist shooting out of the box like the gradual
Appearance of morning at morning like Tutankhamen
Carefully divesting death in public places.

13.
I achieved apocalypse—hearing slowly the sounds
Against which my ears had made their own music.

I heard first the Rhondda choral echo up the valley
Trying to find god's ear, I heard the presage
Ironically rumbling along the Channel, war:
The ancestral voice, the ancestral voice. And
I saw in a fog of gas Mr. Baldwin orating:
We must repair the deficiencies of our forces.
I heard three women weeping in Irun's ruins.

14.
Nothing I could not hear, *Berliner*
Tageblatt, *Daily Telegraph*, *L'Humanité*, *Isvestia*,
The air like newsboys shrieking, recounting
Instances of hate, of insult, aggravation, and
The Rhondda choral, the Durham hymn, over all.
I met seven saints in Salisbury with cotton wool in their ears,
I remembered with shame my own music.
The splitting of the central pillar like aural lightning,
I felt it crack my abdomen, the world.

VII.

1.
What when born upward breaking from heaven downward
Brilliantly glittering in the new-born eye, firing
The flame of grace, what when descending on the babe
Terrible in the toil of original sin, shines, showers,
Cleanses, charges, redeems the demeaned divine.
What wink of wonder awakens the soul,
What dove's is the feather I feel under my arm
Rustling and wrestling and rendering me mine?

2.
O world, my white breasted, my cruelly crowned, my singing
Swan of Wyoming, Shropshire, floating through the reflected
Oxford towers, O my multitudinously feathered swan,
Gathering the souls like babes to the breast, my mother
World, murmuring the lark's lullaby and the whippoorwill's
sorrow,
Bearing on your breast the burden of the thousand
Heaven feathers, move idly, move easily, sail like a song
Dipping your wild laboured breast in Time like Thames.

3.
O world, my westward wanderer, my white blackbird, from
whom
To whom wandering, my nonpareil, my phœnix star, I
follow
Where from whence, to whom, to what; unknown, I only
know
I follow my white swan along the dark westward flow,
Gathering the odd few feathers fallen from her breast
Tossed in the dark, lost in the tremendous dark.
I am her consort like the pilot fish,
The Orpheus of her Eurydice.

4.
It was her one note traversing Time
Awoke me in the bower of the womb, I rose
And saw her passing on the dark westward stream,
The myriad of human struggling at her breast.
I saw her sailing like a mirage through the willows
Whose boughs like fruit the flashing worlds encrusted.
Breaking through boughs I made towards her, and behind
Heard a windfall of the Aladdin stars descend.

5.
The green dream hung in the male tree bled when I burst
And burning boy out of the apple I fell.
The womb like apple hangs on the starry tree
Which willow is along the Time-Thames banks.
The bursting apple frees the feathered babe
Who flies and falls at the world's swan breast.
My mother swan of Windsor white and gold,
Was it your swan note split the autumn womb?

VIII.

1.
The wave approaching and the wave returning,
The grave broken and the worm militant,
The myrtle blossoms from the twisted pillar,
Love illuminates the scene of horror.
Inevitably to life consigned,

The flame consuming, the by flame consumed,
Eternally eternally bud and blossom
Evolve the particular of doom.

2.
The paralysed bird within the summer tree
Amber and dumb, I love the silent bird;
The figure in folds of Time attired
Denuded at nativity;
Apples at hand, the apples at the thigh
Love plucked, the girl in feathery garters
Loudly disrobing by the open window—
Though bird is silent life is the word.

3.
The ghost I dug through Twickenham turns round,
I see the bridge involved with its bowels;
The Richmond lady gathering Spring flowers
Reveals the ache of Time like rhododendron
Red in her bosom; the boy with the bright hair
Shows me his guts with the tame mice there.
And I in turn bare the nerve of soul,
They leap in and sleep on the bright curve.

4.
Henceforth wandering with my womb
Heavy with ghost, the Richmond lady, boy,
I hang at finger the tree like toy,
The flower wear like a wonder wound.
Objects revolve, as I proceed,
About my breast like solar system;
With the bleeding eye I bleed,
Event is staged hysteria.

5.
Coerced by music and caressed by blossoms,
The lost, the stolen, and the strayed,
Wandering through the unending colonnade
Show the rhododendrons at their bosoms.
The ache of Time that testifies decay

Ascertains peace; the tired lady
With Richmond flowers in her hair,
Leads me to the vague of nowhere.

6.
Spreadeagled like the full-length mirror,
Pinioned like brilliant butterfly,
Fixed through gold axle on the Ixion sky,
I blaze in vacuum of being's horror.
The shapes of sense, the jerking thigh,
The eye dividing, the hand and hand,
This is the limbo circus of the human,
The man, the idol one, the illustrious I.

7.
The illustrious I with bird at ankle,
The monster of glory in the bowels,
The boy forget-me-not that blows
In the blue eye, and manacled
Through the glass of acts the ghost
Forward at hand: guitar beneath
The lifted tongue, and in the throat
The seventy petals of dahlia death.

8.
The wave approaching and the wave returning,
The opening stone and the worm eternal,
The animal of agony at the groin
Fighting to burst the sex bag of skin;
The giant I, crucified to my spine,
Who stretches and crushes me—I suffer
Seeing the bruises burgeon along the body
Blossom to bring the suffocator rose.

IX.

1.
The centre of the heart like a red tree
Shoots forth a hand pointing towards mirrors.
And when I look I see myself embroiled like
The Egyptian corpse in images of self.

I feel the heavy towelling of space
Wound round my active corpse which is alive
Like bug in vacuum only in itself.
I scratch the itch of self to make it swell.

2.
The rope of glory dangling from heaven held me,
I pulled upon the pulley and day by day
Felt the feet lift and the throttling at the throat,
The clouds of wonder gathering like gas and dope
Shaping and simulating figures of desire and achievement;
I pulled from here with heaven as my lever,
The rope of god throttling me was my guts.

3.
I hear the admonition of the whippoorwill
Wending through woods with fodder on his bosom
Keeping his home though the leopard roars and the lion
Lying low, waits: though the lime like an eye
Mesmerizes and the air faints at danger he flies.
I feel the bird at my eyelids beating to awaken
The free and easy fellow in me, him who
So wide might wander once away from me.

4.
It is the world that called me to come
And I obeyed and left the arbour womb;
It is my mother swan whose cry of song
As it first split the apple in which I lay
Divides the beetle husk of the illustrious I.
And like the phœnix snake from beetle skin
I feel the free one in me move.

5.
The inheritance of chaos I leave him, Love
Only the feathery garter and the girl,
Milton nibbling like a mouse at his window,
And always and always the dope of life, death,
Arriving in letters from the Bay of Naples.
I leave him the lost, the stolen, and the strayed,

The strange, the erratic, the rich, the mad,
I leave him himself, for this was all he had.

6.
The bowels I burst from lying askew about him
Tremble and move and coil like life about him.
The stranglehold they throttle at his throat is
The serpent brood murdering its parent.
He loved himself so much that the act of love
Made with himself, gave him, as hybrid, death.
But phœnix, beetle, snake, from his blood,
I rose and felt the throes of Spain.

7.
Continually the women weeping in Irun's ruins
Call in distress with voices like swans;
I hear that cry which breaks the womb or room
Wherever I stand, and forces me to go.
The swan my world with a myriad at her breast,
The foaming human struggling, I hear their cry;
The feminine weeping and the masculine agony
Meet at the throat and make the swan's song.

8.
Not over the National spoken and not shown at cinema
To blackout Paramount with the facts like lights,
The horror facts, the human in its horror. Derelict
Wales and the Northumberland wastes whose day of dark
Shows better the bare and bony human. How can he cease
From political fight, how can his word sleep in his hand,
When a dark time in a dark time
Inundates and annihilates the mind?

9.
Who is he whom I may not mourn for but me,
My predecessor behind the familiar eye,
The marvellous mathematician who made
The myriad of human mean less than his one.
I mourn him as tomorrow mourns today,
Especially as the sun shines, and summer comes.

I leave him in the wreathes of his bowels.
Self-born, self-fed, self-alive, and self-dead.

10.
I leave him the serpent continually swallowing itself,
I leave him the terrier chasing its tail,
I leave him the martyr in flame for a private cause,
I leave him the love that fears the lunar valley
The sanguinary moon and the breeding amœba,
I leave him his eyes like mirrors
Repeating his image in innumerable recession.
I inherit his hand.

X.

1.
The English coast shivers and the American meadow faints;
The Rhône and the Rhine run mellowing with promised horror;
The Welsh mountain weeps and the Cumberland fell weeps;
London lies like a huge rot along the Thames, and Rome
Roars. O Spain, my golden red, she tears the rot out,
The Franco gangs that furrow in her heart. See how she stands,
Her Madrid middle growing vague with ravage,
Labouring to let out liberty, with the rat and the rot at her heart.

2.
I remember again the three women weeping in Irun's ruins,
Whose tears will wash the Rhône and Rhine and whose grief
Thrust up like crystal towers the architecture of Time.
I see England
With the underground mines run bleeding along her like wounds,
I hear the great Lancastrian shafts delivering sounds
Of sorrow and appeal, or watch the factory stacks
Like hands for charity, or fallen, clenched.

3.
The centre of my heart like a red tree
Puts forth a hand and indicates the common red rose;
Which when I take lifts its petals like tongues
Articulating red; speaks of privations, poverty,
Duplicity, oppressions, camouflaged collusions;

And I observe that every move of its lips leaves blood.
What flower then shall the red tree in my heart wear
But the red tongues of the rose, which speak and bleed?

4.
O Asturias Wyoming and Wales, I see the fuchsia
Remembering man has a crimson heart and I remember,
Hang out my fuchsia here. Your fuchsia, Asturias,
Spreading like sun over Spain shall be soon in bloom:
The dead is dead, but he gives and not takes his poppy,
His hammer his hand and his badge his blood.
It is already time to triumph, for tears and blood like time
Take tears and blood as time takes time to make good.

5.
I see the swan's breast run like the pelican's red
To feed the crowded myriad her human,
I see the large parasites that dilate like leech
Torn, with war and agony, from my mother world's front.
But the whippoorwill wends his way through the Wyoming
 woods
When the leopard, lying low, awaits, or the lion
Roars. And my mother world, with bomb holes in her bosom.
Goes gradually on, with the myriad of me at her breast.

Allegory of the Adolescent and the Adult

It was when weather was Arabian I went
Over the downs to Alton where winds were wounded
With flowers and swathed me with aroma, I walked
Like Saint Christopher Columbus through a sea's welter
Of gaudy ways looking for a wonder.

Who was I, who knows, no one when I started,
No more than the youth who takes longish strides,
Gay with a girl and obstreperous with strangers,

Fond of some songs, not unusually stupid,
I ascend hills anticipating the strange.

Looking for a wonder I went on a Monday,
Meandering over the Alton down and moor;
When was it I went, an hour a year or more,
That Monday back, I cannot remember.
I only remember I went in a gay mood.

Hollyhock here and rock and rose there were,
I wound among them knowing they were no wonder;
And the bird with a worm and the fox in a wood
Went flying and flurrying in front, but I was
Wanting a worse wonder, a rarer one.

So I went on expecting miraculous catastrophe.
What is it, I whispered, shall I capture a creature
A woman for a wife, or find myself a king,
Sleep and awake to find Sleep is my kingdom?
How shall I know my marvel when it comes?

Then after long striding and striving I was where
I had so long longed to be, in the world's wind,
At the hill's top, with no more ground to wander
Excepting downward, and I had found no wonder.
Found only the sorrow that I had missed my marvel.

Then I remembered, was it the bird or worm,
The hollyhock, the flower or the strong rock,
Was it the mere dream of the man and woman
Made me a marvel? It was not. It was
When on the hilltop I stood in the world's wind.

The world is my wonder, where the wind
Wanders like wind, and where the rock is
Rock. And man and woman flesh on a dream.
I look from my hill with the woods behind,
And Time, a sea's chaos, below.

Vision of England '38

I.

I lay, not in Malvern or Alexandra Palace
From where the southern sorrow of the horizon is seen
Encompassing more of misery than a tear's whole circle,
But in Brighton I lay in bed, and behind my head

The tremendous panoply of England fell vertical,
The historical curtain exuding blood on my pillow;
Conspicuously suspended from diamonds of justice
Dredged from the depths of national despair.

Not sleeping not dreaming I saw the imperial procession
Flicker past my foot in postures of triumph or violence;
Some moved in shapes of gluttony or envy, others
Rode pride like lions, and some bore their own flowers.

I heard voices that whispered and voices that sang,
'Death is no glory', or 'I shun not the fire'.
Three women came screaming, wringing hands, flying,
With crowns on their brows, the last of them Victoria.

Behind them, randy as the angry beast who craves
Dominion for its ball and sceptre, loped the Disraelian lion.
The three queens with its scions in their loins
Flew forward screaming, hunting for their graves.

Nor could I halt this parade of historical character,
Not with a lifted hand and a cry, or an electric candle;
Not with appeals or protests or references to authority:
The shuffling crowd streamed through in a bright dream.

O lamentable lips that ragged showed their burns,
As that beautiful youth with Saint Mary Redcliffe in hand
Stepped forward and fell at my side and murmured:
'I warn you, not poison.'

Who took my hand and left an orchid there,
With the mark of his lips that parted their shapes
To speak a word of hope: was it salacious Oscar
Or the lost Orphic who coughed blood at Naples?

'Remember me, remember me,' cried the skull
That floated through with seaweed in its teeth.
'Drowned in a sudden squall I found him there,
Waiting under the wave, God ambushed me there.'

Then I abandoned my attitude of ease on the bed
To touch the salt tear that the skull had shed:
And like a pearl it poised upon my hand, and I
Saw in its circle the temporal Harlequin dome.

Next the rhodomontade of the political opera
Shattered my gaze and daze as I saw enter
The onager, the serpent and the macaw,
Tussling together over the heart of man.

But what one tore or what all three ravaged,
Though the wounds bled, seemed to restore
Soon to its shape like a world after war,
And all that commemorates is the blood on the floor.

So I took Shelley's tear which like a single rain
Dropped into the blood that murmured at my feet:
And a ghost arose holding out its hands in pain,
Looking at me with eyes that supplicated fate.

'From tears and blood I spring in sorrow and anger,
The long anonymous inhabitants of dearth.
I'm Wat Tyler's wife and Robert Owen's lover,
From whom you also came starving at birth.

'Remember me when the rose is too close,
Or when the triumphant dove coos sweetly
Filling the world with love, do not forget me.
I shall be here, the tenant of my woes.'

'Wait,' I said slowly. 'Tell me why I,
Lying at night in my Brighton bed,
Receive the visitation of the conspicuously dead,
Terrifying me with their mad pageantry.'

He lifted his head like a lover to me,
Smiling with a secret that no words revealed:
Then he said softly, 'Mystery is no mystery
When Time divests it of its present mists.

'Therefore wait with patience: you will see
More than the theatrical zodiac of history.
Look closely enough and life will show her source
From higher than Chilterns and a grander course.'

Then the rain tatooed the window. He was gone,
Leaving me alone in a room of time
So small that I filled it with a minute sigh,
For the host and the ghost were gone.

II.

But I arose, with a star against my cheek
Roaring of winter with the tongues of Orion:
'The great winds rage in the mane of the lion,
But not great winds make the lion weak.'

Near me the sea in nocturnal lamentation
Shrouded itself in hoods and wept a shower,
Retreating in sorrow from the lion's locks
Where he lies emaciated on capital rocks.

Cassiopeia wept. I felt her brilliant sympathy
Falling upon me as I walked by the waves;
I looked up at her outstretched arms in the sky
Too far to reach me and too near for a grave.

Then a saint walked up out of the sea,
Dragging his death behind him like a boat

He had a rusty sword and he said to me:
'I killed an enormous monster, but the brute

'Still rules England with its scales of gold.
O my green girl given to the rape of the banker,
The careerist politician and the vague thinker,
Lie easy for one more night out in the cold.'

He gave me his sword with a long look,
Then turned, and returned to his death.
I glanced down at the iron in my hand, and found
The blueblooded point that bleeds a book.

So I lay down against Saint George's green girl
To keep her warm an hour in my arms.
To see us lying by the waves' whirl
The dove also wept among the Great Dog's curls.

But Peace is dear and cannot be bought with sleep,
Any more than Birmingham can keep peace in steel:
So as I lay between a dream and a sleep
A tongue licked me, and I saw it was a sheep.

'This green,' it said, 'this pleasant place,
Not yet is fit for the foot of Christ.
How can your word or your sword sleep
While the Thames is the sweat of the people?

'I am Blake who broke my mind on God.
I tell you he does not touch this world
Till the disease is scoured from the sod
By the blood of wrong made fit for his hand.'

The touch of the tongue as the Lamb kissed
Fired my spirit with the bliss of fate
When the spirit senses the great ultimate
To which it toils through mystery and mist.

Alone on the dark beach I stood.
The teeth of the seas tore the shore.

'O immensely sad land,' I said, 'where
Only the ghosts are good.'

III.

I ride my grief along the road
Leaving the littoral cities to their summer sins;
Brighton and Bournemouth with the pots of God
Brimming fire over the signs of the times.

But who could whistle or sing in the South
With its ramshackle witch-barns broken and ruined;
Where the disused thresher rusts among the lichens,
And the brood scuttles in the kitchens?

So I went northward to Salisbury on Friday.
But on the bridge I encountered a figure
Who crossed me with a look and shook his head:
'It's market day but even so we are dead.'

'I'm William Longspée who lies in stone
In the north aisle of the Cathedral:
All the semblance of Salisbury's life is a pall
Covering the famous faces of the dead and gone.

'There's nothing here but the mere loveliness
Of the long lost Gothic ache to heaven:
Like the lily in which the dead dress,
Salisbury is a beautiful funeral.'

And I saw the sweet alto of the spire sing upward
Like the long note of the God-mourning choir
Creating a tomb of music, or song's pyre
Over the bones of Salisbury in Wiltshire.

From the Bay of Swanage as I came down in Dorset
The shade of Alfred arose shaking a guilty hand;
He pointed westward to Weymouth and with a hoarse voice
Cried: 'See what a fatal gift I gave England!'

Manœuvring over the broad water like gnats
The naval seaplanes and the giant cruisers
Spread their shadows over the boats and bathers
Who played in Weymouth Bay among the shadows.

Then I saw that they floated in blood and blossoms,
The blood of the bathers, the blossoms of the boughs
That made the boats: under the dreadnought bosoms
Crushed and bruised under the huge bows.

Alfred arraigned. 'O my people, what have I done
Unto thee, unto thee! O Arthur, Arthur!
Go, boy, over to Glastonbury and ask for Arthur,
Ask there for Arthur. Say England needs a father.'

He struck the Georgian Memorial in the street with his hand
As I strike nettles, and left it in the gutter.
He sprang in the trough of a wave and floated away.
Went down muttering with his face in his hands.

And I heard the air full of the songs of swans.
So I went down westward to Abbotsbury, whose waters
Echo so many ends that here the swan's valediction
Dies in the morning and is never dead.

It is the native music of contemporary England
I reflected when wandering along the verge;
And awakens in me a music I understand,
The note of the swan who bleeds for her purge.

And though the purge shall bleed her in revolution,
Dry up her unhappy heart whence song arises,
Rupture that loveliness with mechanical contortion,
If she achieves her perfect peace, it is the prize.

IV.

North also to the broad vowels and the mountains,
Leaving the melancholy swans who mourn for the nation,

I went towards Mount Rydal where the exhausted fountain
Gaped dry and salty over Wordsworth's memorial.

Here the sun detonated among Cumberland cymbals,
Reminding me of time and my own shadow:
How soon I shall lie easy, evaded the shambles,
The tremendous pendulum of the stars and my own sorrow.

But then from the ground it arose, my shade,
Bearing the teeth that shook in my own jaw:
'I am you. Forget me. No more me. No more
Dallying with the Idalian in the glade.'

He swung his arm to the east, and there
Down the mountain path came a young woman,
Wearing a tawdry blouse and careless hair,
Who hurried as though pursued by a rumour.

'He's behind me! He's behind me!' she cried, running.
Then I caught her hand and drew her from the road.
'Who?'—and the pulse of her hand, drumming,
Answered, 'Fear is abroad! Fear is abroad!'

'I am the North,' she said, 'whom the South follows
Like bailiff or police who demand my money.
He caught me on the road and rifled my mine,
Took the gold from my teeth and left me hollow.

'Yes, the South in his bowler and morning jacket,
His leather satchel, and handkerchief in pocket,
He called me a whore, but when he'd had his worth
Not a penny he paid me for the child I bring forth.'

She ran her hand through her hair. I saw
Jarrow on her third finger like a lead ring.
'Yes,' she said, 'he absconded after the war,
The husband for whom I wore flowers in the spring.

'Write it red in your lines, O write it red,
I starve with my children on the northern seaboard.

Warn well the pot-bellied and the over-fed,
I'll have their hearts to fill my echoing cupboard.'

Then the December star sprang over a rock,
Filling the lines of her face with livid silver;
And a filigree of lace flittered over her shoulder,
Making her anger a monument of silver.

'Nevertheless Venus is lovely,' I said,
And heard Wordsworth turn over in his grave:
Windermere flashed in my face at the words,
Where it hung at her eye instead.

'Go down. Go down. The eagle's eyrie,
The angel's angle, the abandoned wife's hearth,
These are no places for the nose of the query.
Leave me to birth.'

But beside Windermere I shall move at night
When the West Wind blows into my window
The tresses of Venus where they wave their light,
Even though I come from a dream of splendour.

Not less strong than the indomitable rock,
Not less lovely than the lake and the star,
The wife of England roves in the North,
Among the derelict cities and the memories of war.

V.

Last in the Eastern Marshes I made a way
From town to town over the bog and slough,
Where the quartz cathedrals guide the stray
Like pillars in plains or pins in cloth:

With against my left ear the advancing sea
Gnawing the shore near Cromer, and water
Fallen around like glass, where tulips brought
A false sunrise, here I could see

The angel of stone in the attitude of song
Flicked with a tint of gilt above Norwich;
But its story only asked that the city be made rich,
More gilt and glory and less right and wrong.

And a fox over Cambridge and a fish over Yarmouth
Yapping and yawing for cash and credit:
Everywhere here I saw the larks of youth
Tethered to banks for a debit.

Then a sad yammering wormed along the air
Like underground mouths swarming in the sky, and I
Heard from the south arise like the rumour of despair,
The moan of the seven million in the capital city.

O London, magnificent monster in whose guts
The bishop lisps with notes and the poet writes
With penny words, whose hunger cannot glut
With glory or gluttony, on whom a world waits,

I saw you astride the South in coils
Of insatiable economic appetite:
Mauling the Sussex hills and the broad
Hampshire heath for a maudlin profit.

Where is the Cappadocian for that throat
To cut the health and wealth of England loose?
O Political Prince, from this rock release
The national man and woman, who groan!

I see him rise sweating from the North,
Up from the deep shaft or the steel yard:—
He comes down not drummed or crowned or starred,
But nevertheless inheritor of the earth.

O equitable stars hasten that liberation!

The Death of Yeats

That dolphin-torn, that gong-tormented face
With the trumpets of Andromeda rose and spoke,
Blaring the pitiful blast and airing hope
So hope and pity flourished. Now the place
Cold is where he was, and the gold face
Shimmers only through the echoes of a poem.

The swan mourns on the long abandoned lake,
And on the verge gather the great Irish ghosts
Whom only he could from their myth awaken
And make a kingdom. The luckless and the lost
Got glory from the shake of his hand as he passed,
The lunar emperor whom Time could not break.

The boulder where he rested his shoulder is
Luckier than most, who know nothing of
The tremendous gentleness of the poet's kiss,
Thwarted by passion and impelled by love.
But the lost leaf lashed in a March above
Shares sense of action that is also his.

Saints on mountains or animals in the ground
Often found the feather of his wing on their lips
Proving and loving them; stars in their eclipse
Saw his face watching through intervening ground:
And the small fry like fish came up at the sound
Of his voice and listened to his whistling lips.

But now the cloud only shall hear: the ant,
The winter bulb under the ground, and the hidden
Stream be made dumb by his murmur in death,
Lying between the rock and the jealous plant.
No matter how close to the ground I bend, his breath
Is not for me, and all divisions widen.

Remember the lion's head and the blonde angel
Whispering in the chimney; remember the river

Singing sweeter and sweeter as it grows older and older;
Remember the moon sees things from a better angle.
O forget the echoes that go on for ever,
And remember that the great harp-breasted eagle
Is now a grave.

Triumphal Ode Mcmxxxix

Through the green tassels of the weeper tree,
When idle in the evening I walk down by the river,
Risen to its zenith in my pessimism's heaven
I see the red star tremendous in the South—
Turning the Thames an aorta of war, turning
Red the left cheek of Venus, and my gaze
Forward to autumn through the gases' haze.
Then at my side I hear the tree weep
Its sweat of tears like pearls into the water,
With the sound of drums and the nasal trumpet
Muffled by grief to an echo; no, not the weeper
Is a green tree but my mother in a hood
Leaning over the years intervening between
Belgium's bugle and the Polish disaster.
Or at my feet summer sheds its blood
In sacrificial glory on my senses' altar,
Blazing Time's aisle with Helianthus standards,
Hanging the tombs with poppies: Time shall have tombs,
Time shall have too many tombs for summer's banners
To ornament with the oriflammes of its blossoms.
Over my head the lonely lark spins
Dizzy with cadenzas trailing from the tail feathers,
Goes up for joy and comes down for pleasure,
A shuttlecock of rapture,
No longer lonely among the clouds, no longer
Chases its echoes up the sky's corridor—
The roar of the thousand horses of the bomber
Is louder among the clouds of its own anger.
Against my knee the fern brushes its fans

Or nods its osprey crests against my hand,
Like a tame creature made quiet by its name:
I move among its plumes, and as I stand
Autumn comes over and renders into flame
The general green: the white feathers, tinged
Are singed by the red star with absurd shame.
And at my cheek the southern zephyr,
Coy as a curl, makes its amorous comments,
Remembered from moments over the Coast of Azure,
When like a dove it hovered over the lovers:
And I could listen, but the kisses of my leisure,
As, with eyes closed, I stoop to meet that mouth—
Then my lids will not lift from the dead seizure
Struck on my senses by Mars in the South.

Then at my face the shower of rain
Stardusts me with a handful of its brilliants,
Flecking my lashes like worlds: the violence
Of winds may shake them, but only fall for pain.
Temperate is the weather of all other worlds,
But ours is red at morning, as the dawn
Comes glittering with obituaries; on the wolds
The rain falls from those other worlds that mourn
To see the pain.
To see the pain I cannot raise my gaze
Forwards towards the autumnal calendar,
Where, like a figure numbering the days,
Bleeds a flesh wound down the face of paper
Commemorating the catastrophe of the future.
Nor can I sleep, for in my sleep
At my left side, nearest to the heart,
Press close the rows of everlasting sleepers
Laid on my bed by the mad hand of hate
With a bag of dirt in their mouths. O keep
Quieter their sleep than mine, not loud with planes,
Nor let them hear in the booth of their deep
Silence, the ringing bells of pain
Rolling and tolling all night and all day.
Yet we shall enter the time of ghosts,
Where those once known hang about in corners

Whispering to us their praises of the past,
The picnics, the gay dances, the sweet stories;
And I among them, jostling their shoulder-bones,
Feel on the back of my hand the evening mist
Of their mourning fall, or drop its water stones
To crush their memories.

This is the year that must be memorable
Not for its crop of corn or its fine weather,
Not for its anniversaries but rather
Memorable for the terrible star in the South,
The badge of war. Slow, slow the stellar cycles,
To give us longer the minutes of our youth
And hold the kiss of Psyche
Under the glare of Mars in a time of ruth.

Truth is the mirage after which we labour
Through wastes of pain under destruction's star,
Which, though we cannot reach or in it harbour,
Teaches us that our resting-place is far
Further than New Zealand or a nebula.

Holy Poems

C. B. IN MEMORIAM. JUNE, MCMXXXIX

I.

i.

Nimrod, hung like God's scalp on Time's bosom,
Warns me without words to keep from blood.
Mad blood like a red wave drives my raft
Against the fang of fate, the tooth of doom.
Turn back the mad tides of the time with Truth
Whose moon can move the seas behind the breast
With a wink of wonder or a gaze of God.

ii.
Siamese monster of Christ and the Devil
I coil my sins in ecstasy around me:
Bound in the centre, martyred to my evil,
Burning with yearning the God I in me
Melts like a candle of tears to see
Satan triumphant at one side of me.
O my left side where Hell inhabits me!

iii.
Andromeda world, fixed to God's rock,
Who, what am I to drop down from the sky
Shaking a word's sword, capped with a rose,
Booted with birds and gloved with love,
To crack that world and free a world:
The dove that nestles in the green breast,
O world within a world!

iv.
Tamburlaine makes a magnificent mushroom
Rotten in the home of the bone with a worm:
But though no more than a spot of rot, he knows
More than I know, the holy name and home.
Tamburlaine, tongue in a field, tell, tell,
What's God's prefix, and shall I find a room
Made for the mad, ready for me in Hell?

v.
Tamburlaine, tell, the galaxy-barred sky
Does not make gaol or cage the bird:
I mean the body's lodger bird that goes home
When a wound or a sorrow lets him fly?
He is free there? He is easy? Who takes him
Light on the palm of his hand in the mornings,
Makes him to twitter and preen and sing?

vi.
Narcissus, embalmed in glass and rivers,
Speaks to me with the lisp of the tides;
Murmurs to me late in the summer evenings

When he goes down with the last fish, whispers:
'The kiss of doom is death. So deep a kiss,
No love knows as the hermaphrodite worm:
With it I lie always at the sex of bliss,
And this is loss.'

vii.
Venus, naked against the face of the day,
Is my sweet star. I watch it tip the sky
Like a nude beauty posing on a rock
Trembling at winds and at the waves' hands—
Shake, my evening Venus, in the coral clouds!
I not so fine and not so vivid whistle
Of heaven also to a cloud of crowd.

II.

The Seven Seas with their angel-infested crests
Circumscribe and symbolize a world that never rests,
Whistling and swinging down a recurring West.

In the red theatre of the flesh I stage
The anatomical tragedy of this sad age
Whose sweat of tears cannot put out rage.

Now the guns rock my vision as I look
With blood-prognosticating eyes on Europe
Whose weeping map invades all my books.

Not if I mourn the Tussaud comedy stops
To halt the funeral that descends the steps
Which only Love can with a great gaze stop.

O Europe with Imperial Eagles on its peak,
None can climb but perish on the apex of
Pride, is not the high world that I seek.

But ride instead the angel-infested wave,
Attesting that a mystery crowns our lives
With the smile of God's blood-flecked jaws.

Therefore I look with Love, Gaze, great heart,
On this inhuman fury until the blaze of hate
Creates itself the martyrdom of fate.

Then with a shout I shall leap out
Among the loud angel-infested crowd;
And, whistling, show the glory of my shroud.

III.

Truant too long from the booth of the tomb
Where bells rejoice bringing God's voice to me,
I run amuck among the ragamuffin roads
Chasing the rainbow for an hour of glory.
And the evangelists singing in the streets
Tell me of hell wherever I go for happiness—
Admonish me with the music of my own bones
Blown by Gabriel for a maroon of warning.

O blow my bone loud, O Gabriel, so I hear
God rolling and tolling down the avenues,
Telling me with a terrible bell Hell is my diurnal:
Beatitude all about me builds a tomb of amber
Where I shall lie like butterfly, embedded in revelation
Of its ephemeral its eternal wings. O songs
No less than the Chrysostom firefly be.

Blow my bone loud, O Gabriel— drive me from
The river where I laze among memories,
Lying and gazing at the distorted form
Below me in the water: love above and under
But no love in between. O blow me home,
Waft home my boat with winds of rage,
But let my imagination's haemorrhage
Trail scarlet lake the message of my dreams.

Now when I walk in the street
Truant I am anticipating trumpets:
When the mad train at night shoots up its scream
I turn around to see God in His thunder

Come riding cowboy downward on my shoulder,
Or watch the flying angel of the steam
Gold-feathered, fire-bowelled, wink an eye
Warning me it is nearly time to say good-bye.

Not yet, not yet. But eager at the corner
I stand with an ear cocked for the bugle.
So the brass trombone of the beggar
Blasts my eardrums with terror of tomorrow:
The Avalon haven I have in the grave
Is now death-haunted by God like Arthur—
So when I shall the last time close my eye
O God will smother me like a father
Mothering the son still hanging in his thigh.

IV.

i.
I am Saint John on Patmos of my heart
Towered and tabernacled with illusion;
Black Michaels and gold Satans stand at hand
Gulling me with their gestures of temptation
To bring me down from the marvellous mountains
Where in Babylonian gardens I find
Spinoza's face hanging from every tree
Murmuring love of all our kith and kind:
Or I feel, cold as a daught on my arm,
The spiralling universe like a worm
Coiling for comfort; and in my mind
The three-winged dove among my dreams
Moaning for its apocalyptic home.

ii.
I bleed Sebastian's brother on the ground,
No good it does me: or I hang my hand
My harp-hand on the Haman tree, but no—
My blood smiles from the ground in pride,
My hand makes music when winds blow.
There is no martyrdom worse than a life,
Nor can it be bought off with a sacrifice.

I cannot cut my body to Saint Peter's key,
Or, nipping off the hip-rose with a knife
Make me archangel, nor with a kiss
Claim thirty shillings, for no one will buy
The plaster Jesus that my master is,
Crossed on my pain and crucified in my eye.

iii.
The monarch who wears a shrieking crown
Is us. All whipping tongues and words
Flash at our head and doom us down:
The sex of our cherubim is swords.
When we step down out of our beds or doors
The burning bush springs up between our feet;
Our smile is bright with tiger, and the days
Turn us like dogs in their drums. Then comes
Spinning and shining among us like wheels,
Throwing off visions to lead us home,
God—snatches me up in finger and thumb,
Douses me like a glimmer. And I see
Cruel to be kind to all his kind is he.

'O Who will speak from a Womb or a Cloud?'

Not less light shall the gold and the green lie
On the cyclonic curl and diamonded eye, than
Love lay yesterday on the breast like a beast.
Not less light shall God tread my maze of nerve
Than that great dread of tomorrow drove over
My maze of days. Nor less terrible that tread
Stomping upon your grave than I shall tread there.
Who is a god to haunt the tomb but Love?

Therefore I shall be there at morning and midnight,
Not with a straw in my hair and a tear as Ophelia
Floating along my sorrow, but I shall come with
The cabala of things, the cipher of nature, so that

With the mere flounce of a bird's feather crest
I shall speak to you where you sit in all trees,
Where you conspire with all things that are dead.
Who is so far that Love cannot speak to him?

So that no corner can hide you, no autumn of leaves
So deeply close over you that I shall not find you,
To stretch down my hand and sting you with life
Like poison that resurrects. O remember
How once the Lyrae dazzled and how the Novembers
Smoked, so that blood burned, flashed its mica,
And that was life. Now if I dip my hand in your grave
Shall I find it bloody with autumn and bright with stars?
Who is to answer if you will not answer me?

But you are the not yet dead, so cannot answer.
Hung by a hair's breadth to the breath of a lung,
Nothing you know of the hole over which you hang
But that it's dark and deep as tomorrow midnight.
I ask, but you cannot answer except with words
Which show me the mere interior of your fear,
The reverse face of the world. But this,
This is not death, the standing on the head
So that a sky is seen. O who
Who but the not yet born can tell me of my bourne?

Lie you there, lie you there, my never, never,
Never to be delivered daughter, so wise in ways
Where you perch like a bird beyond the horizon,
Seeing but not being seen, above our being?
Then tell me, shall the meeting ever be,
When the corpse dives back through the womb
To clasp his child before it ever was?
Who but the dead can kiss the not yet born?

Sad is space between a start and a finish,
Like the rough roads of stars, fiery and mad.
I go between birth and the urn, a bright ash
Soon blazed to blank, like a fire-ball. But
Nothing I bring from the before, no message,

No clue, no key, no answer. I hear no echo,
Only the sheep's blood dripping from the gun,
The serpent's tear like fire along the branch.
O who will speak from a womb or a cloud?

Epistle I

Meeting a monster of mourning wherever I go
Who crosses me at morning and evening also,
For whom are you miserable I ask and he murmurs
I am miserable for innumerable man: for him
Who wanders through Woolworth's gazing at tin stars;
I mourn the maternal future tense, Time's mother,
Who has him in her lap, and I mourn also her,
Time whose dial face flashes with scars.

I gave the ghost my money and he smiled and said,
Keep it for the eyeballs of the dead instead.
Why here, I asked, why is it here you come
Breaking into the evening line going to another,
Edging your axe between my pencil fingers,
Twisting my word from a comedy to a crime?
I am the face once seen never forgotten,
Whose human look your dirty page will smother.

I know what it was, he said, that you were beginning;
The rigmarole of private life's belongings.
Birth, boyhood, and the adolescent baloney. So I say
Good go ahead, and see what happens then.
I promise you horror shall stand in your shoes,
And when your register of youth is through
What will it be but about the horror of man?
Try telling about birth and observe the issue.

Epping Forest where the deer and girls
Mope like lost ones looking for Love's gaols—
Among the dilapidated glades my mother wandered
With me as a kid, and sadly we saw

The deer in the rain near the trees, the leaf-hidden shit,
The Sunday papers, and the foliage's falling world;
I not knowing nothing was our possession,
Not knowing Poverty my position.

Epping Forest glutted with the green tree
Grew up again like a sweet wood inside me.
I had the deer browsing on my heart,
This was my mother; and I had the dirt.
Inside was well with the green well of love,
Outside privation, poverty, all dearth.
Thus like the pearl I came from hurt,
Like the prize pig I came from love.

Now I know what was wanting in my youth,
It was not water or a loving mouth.
It was what makes the apple-tree grow big,
The mountain fall, and the minnow die.
It was hard cash I needed at my root.
I now know that how I grew was due
To echoing guts and the empty bag—
My song was out of tune for a few notes.

Oh, my ghost cried, the charming chimes of coincidence!
I was born also there where distress collects the rents.
Guttersnipe gutless, I was planted in your guts there,
The tear of time my sperm. I rose from
The woe-womb of the want-raped mind,
Empty hunger cracked with stomach's thunder.
Remembering the rags that flattered your frame
Froze hard and formed this flesh my rind.

So close over the chapter of my birth,
Blessed by distress, baptized by dearth.
How I swung myself from the tree's bough
Demonstrating death in my gay play:
How the germ of the sperm of this ghost like a worm
I caught from the cold comfort of never enough.
How by being miserable for myself I began,
And now am miserable for the mass of man.

Epistle II

Time is not quick enough, space is not far enough,
But I can hit it with the point of my hand.
Now as you sit by a window and watch the bough
Struggling to catch your eye in America, I
Move my right hand, and that is it in England.
The kin of things is deeper and stranger than species:
Kind calls to more than kind, as when I see
The breaking sea that souses me with tears,
Or the lost dog, with whose eyes I stare
Pity. Here in London with winter
Wild at the window I call the Connecticut crow
Mourning my misery on your twig, and he
Calls you: hear how he blows his oboe,
Whose bore is the gouge in my mind agony made.
So deep a note, so large a wound.
I watch you with rain's fall of myriad eyes
Going to shops or shivering for a bus; I touch
Terror at your teeth with a finger's flash.
Whatever my message is, that I cannot write,
Things signify, that speak in the code of life
Not to a tongue translated. And they ask,
Pity, befriend me. Whenever a wonder
Rings the bells in your chamber, remember
My heart strings pull, or I am hit.
Yesterday was it you who gave me hope
When I was walking in Saint Stephen's evening
And saw success luxurify a tree? What thing
Deserves my blood spotted like lepoard's rubies
Excepting this I write? O my leopard-tree
Sprung like a Spring's gem on Shepherd's
Bush Green! Was the west wind you
That forced my sorrow backward,
Drove the tear down my throat? Was all this you
Stretching a hand like a liner over Atlantic
As this line stretches to catch you for a moment
Like telescope star, or forecast catching future?
You see me at this table—what I see

Looks like a mask, an avid womb, a woman,
Swinging together in sunlight from a lintel.
It's you. I tell by the passion of the dead mask,
The dearth of the avid womb, the man in the woman.
What these swing from, mask, womb and woman,
Is door of death's cell, in which life hangs,
And I, too, twisting, hang—
Echo of a tongue, rag of a robe. This line,
This flick of a hand that touches your mask,
Is letter of speech never to be spoken.

The noon now leans at five across my window:
Stands still at noon on yours like a flag pole.
The rag I fixed across it here
Flaps at your window like a hand.
What was the badge it bore, the sign of mine,
Sprawling to warn you wherever you are?
What was the crest I pinned on the day's mast
To take a word of warning or of love to you?
Oh, it was only a word you and I use,
Not knowing what, or why, or how:—
Something like 'love' or 'life'—not to be known,
Not to be understood, not to have meaning more
Than a vague instinct. Then I think of Love
Labouring like a gull in a gale, that keeps
The boat below he follows, or how Love's
Bloody male prow drove into the wave's cleft,
Or the dove dying on the God-forsaken tree.
The tremor in the bone of San Francisco
As the Golden Gate caved in, it cuts
My limbs to square me off like stone, is Life.

Day dupes me and the night converts me.
Night has no meaning in the day, nor has
'Life' meaning, merely accumulation of moods
Like photographs gone faded folded in stacks
Making a mimic tomb of cards, enshrining
A ghost that is gone. I send to you
Not love, not love, but what's between us—space.
Space greater than distances, like that between

The phœnix and its queen, the space that makes
Mountains and lakes and seas, the space that makes
Sorrow and shadow by separation, makes
Things like the bird that flies and falls from grace.
And makes, what's more, men move about and be
Like lines merely measuring paper. I send space
That lies between us and that this flies over:
The space that means to be when it's all over.
Day is dead, it is dark, I am near
The elbow of a dream leaning over,
Reflecting on my page, like me. It is—
It is that Life standing at my shoulder
Silently protesting I have not done it justice.
For, it repeats, there is no space between
The Connecticut crow on the American sill
And that bird tethered to my writing finger:
Look closer, they're the same. Look closer still
And see Connecticut hidden under my hand,
Just as my hand is hidden under that sill.
Then, as I turn to catch Life's face, it's gone.
After it all, what shall I ask, or what answer?
I dare give you nothing but the shapes I make
Like a fish twisting on the Deauville shore
That leaves the lines of life slithered in sand,
The tortured twistings of a headless hand.
So these lines leave my mark, and I leave
The long off you to read them like the magician
Who sees life in the cards or stars, or in a chicken's entrails.

Battersea Park

To Anne Ridler

Now it is November and mist wreathes the trees,
The horses cough their white blooms in the street,
Dogs shiver and boys run; the barges on the Thames
Lie like leviathans in the fog; and I meet

A world of lost wonders as I loiter in the haze
Where fog and sorrow cross my April days.

I recollect it was so often thus; with
Diamonds and pearls like mineral water pointing
The Park railings and the gardens' evergreens:
I spent my winters in summer's disappointments.
The things that burned so bright in my Augusts
Scattering me with their November dusts.

Now I marvel that I am again investigating
The fringes of the bare gardens in the winter.
I had expected to be otherwhere now,
Where the worm coils about the bone's splinter.
Now what good is the great world where I walk
That only revives desire to live once more?

How in the fog of failure and distress
Glitter of things seen in a flicker can
Paralyse will and deter determination,
Make a man afraid of the ghost of a man.
It is the wile of the world of crystal things
That catch the eye and keep me in their rings.

What I saw was Sorrow loitering along by
The Thames near the tall bridge by Battersea Park;
He had in his hand Pavlova or a swan,
And I heard him singing softly in the dark:
My twin, he sang to me, whatever of thine
Is sad and sorry, shall be glad of mine.

And he went on, singing a gay tune.
And now I know that the sorrow is this,
Not that the world a space of sorrow is
But that it's glad. O so gay a grief!
How can I ever be at home here
Where Sorrow sings of Joy in my ears?

How can I ever be happy here, where
Cock robin whistles with a gun at his breast;

Here where the flower has for bud a tear,
Here where Beauty breeds fodder for the Beast?
How can I here be happy, when I know
I can be happy only here and now?

Elegy No. 1

Those occasions involving the veering of axles
When the wheel's bloody spikes like Arabian armaments
Release Passchendaele on us because it is time, bring
Also with blood to the breast the boon to the bosom:
I saw it happen, had near me the gun and the tear.
Those occasions are all elegiac. The wheel and the wish
Turn in a turtle the chaos of life. It is death,
Death like roulette turning our wish to its will.

I see a scene with a smother of snow over Love.
I know Spring will arise and later the swallow return;
I know, but my torso stands bogged in a load of time,
Like Love lying under the smother of our death and our
Dread. How soon shall the Spring bird arise and the
Summer bells hum with the murmur of our name?
            Soon, soon,
Soon the green room goes blue with the last autumn.

I sip at suicide in bedrooms or dare pessimistic stars,
Keep pigeons with messages or make tame apes
Commemorate in mime the master me who must go;
Or commit crimes of rage or rape to ease the ache:
I promise these cannot propitiate fate. No,
Tomorrow it is not, it is not today, it is not
Wednesday or Thursday. It is the greatest day.

That morning not the rose shall rise or dog dance,
Kings with conscience and queens with child sleep long,
For duty is useless; the soldier and sailor glance
Down at their guns with a grin, but they are wrong.

The dodo shall rule for a moment, and the Thames
Remember. Invalids and paralytics shall sing,
'No more, no more!'
I shall hear the ceremony of heaven and God's roar.

What awaits is the veer of the lever and wheel
When the hands cross at midnight and noon, and the future
Sweeps on with a sigh—but on this occasion Time
Swells like a wave at a wall and bursts to eternity.
I await when the engine of lilies and lakes and love
Reaching its peak of power blows me sky high, and I
Come down to rest
On the shape I made in the ground where I used to lie.

O widow, do not weep, do not weep! Or wife
Cry in the corner of the window with a child by—
Look how Tottenham and the Cotswolds, with
More mass than a man, lie easy under the sky,
Also awaiting change they cannot understand.
'I have heaven a haven in my hand,' say,
Like the boy
Cornering butterflies or nothing in cupped hands.

The tragedy is Time foreshadowing its climax.
Thus in the stage of time the minor moth is small
But prophesies the Fokker with marvellous wings
Mottled with my sun's gold and your son's blood.
The crazy anthropoid crawls on time's original
That casts his giant on the contemporary scene:
That spreadeagled shadow
Covers with horror the green Abyssinian meadow.

Lovers on Sunday in the rear seats of cinemas
Kiss deep and dark, for is it the last kiss?
Children sailing on swings in municipal parks
Swing high, swing high into the reach of the sky,
Leave, leave the sad star that is about to die.
Laugh, my comedians, who may not laugh again—
Soon, soon,
Soon Jeremiah Job will be walking among men.

Elegy No. 2

But among the broken glasses and the ticking of the gramophone,
From the divans where sex spread an odour of late last night
Disturbing the collection of fashionable periodicals, yes
          Life like Aphrodite rises;
Scattering tomorrows and shattering yesterdays, rises,
Rises from the cushions on which my youth has died,
          Promising impossible prizes
She dares me to swear that she is the one who will die.

But I shall take her through the autumnal orchards
Where apples like dried worms dangle from the branches;
Or to the cornfield where the barking tractor has
Shorn off the glory of auburn July: or show her
The waiter magpie yesterday picking up tanners
Now dead on my lawn, a gorgeous mess of feathers.
          But she will lift her hand
Defeating funerals with a mere flourish of fingers.

What cyst of poison drips on to my heart that
So soon the mad spectacle of monstrosities in motion
Turns to a carnival, all joy and light, in a moment?
          I regard the neutral stars
Now casting their chaplet of light on the Channel,
Spangling my trees with October's prophecies:
          O pirouetting Pavlovas
Who fill heaven with the dying Swans of Peace!

Also my Hibernian heart, gone with the winter swallow
Returns with the first imitation May morning and poises
Improvising too happy rhapsodies upon my shoulders,
          Gulled at Time's feint:
So I spring up in April joy from December,
As over my head I hear the dancers of fata morgana
Clashing their tambourines in anticipation:
          Tomorrow is carnival.

Thus alternate day and dark that when I lie
Like evening Venus naked on the fall of day,
Life is false planes shimmering in shadows
To which I fade when sleep shuts down my shade.
          O bogus fire
Like the gold glow-worm guiding me to dangers
I'll be the moth who finds a phœnix in fire:
          My to be dead desire.

If I could penetrate future with a false alarm,
      Whom should I raise from lazybone tombs
      But those whom I most love and most harm?
No, for I should bring to them other times,
      The remembrance of remoter themes;
      I could not so dazzle with their dreams
      My eternal yearners for other homes.

Resolution of Dependence

We poets in our youth begin in gladness
But thereof come in the end despondency and madness.
WORDSWORTH: *Resolution and Independence.*

I encountered the crowd returning from amusements,
The Bournemouth Pavilion, or the marvellous gardens,
The Palace of Solace, the Empyrean Cinema: and saw
William Wordsworth was once, tawdrily conspicuous,
Obviously emulating the old man of the mountain-moor,
Traipsing along on the outskirts of the noisy crowd.

Remarkable I reflected that after all it is him.
The layers of time falling continually on Grasmere Churchyard,
The accumulation of year and year like calendar,
The acute superstition that Wordsworth is after all dead,
Should have succeeded in keeping him quiet and cold.
I resent the resurrection when I feel the updraft of fear.

But approaching me with a watch in his hand, he said:
'I fear you are early; I expected a man; I see
That already your private rebellion has been quelled.
Where are the violent gestures of the individualist?
I observe the absence of the erratic, the strange;
Where is the tulip, the rose, or the bird in hand?'

I had the heart to relate the loss of my charms,
The paradise pets I kept in my pocket, the bird,
The tulip trumpet, the penis water pistol;
I had the heart to have mourned them, but no word.
'I have done little reading,' I murmured, 'I have
Most of the time been trying to find an equation.'

He glanced over my shoulder at the evening promenade.
The passing people, like Saint Vitus, averted their eyes:
I saw his eyes like a bent pin searching for eyes
To grip and catch. 'It is a species,' he said,
'I feel I can hardly cope with—it is ghosts,
Trailing, like snails, an excrement of blood.

'I have passed my hand like a postman's into them;
The information I dropped in at once dropped out.'
'No,' I answered, 'they received your bouquet of daffodils,
They speak of your feeling for Nature even now.'
He glanced at his watch. I admired a face.
The town clock chimed like a cat in a well.

'Since the private rebellion, the personal turn,
Leads down to the river with the dead cat and dead dog,
Since the single act of protest like a foggy film
Looks like women bathing, the Irish Lakes, or Saint Vitus,
Susceptible of innumerable interpretations,
I can only advise a suicide or a resolution.'

'I can resolve,' I answered, 'if you can absolve.
Relieve me of my absurd and abysmal past.'
'I cannot relieve or absolve—the only absolution
Is final resolution to fix on the facts.

I mean more and less than Birth and Death; I also mean
The mechanical paraphernalia in between.

'Not you and not him, not me, but all of them.
It is the conspiracy of five hundred million
To keep alive and kick. This is the resolution,
To keep us alive and kicking with strength or joy.
The past's absolution is the present's resolution.
The equation is the interdependence of parts.'

Poem on Ireland

To Margaret Taaffe

My mother reminds me that my birth line,
Accompanying undersea cables, carries
From London back to a Drogheda origin.
Being born in England, like miscarriages
In tubes and taxis, means nothing, for my home
Is there by the Boyne, where never I
Have bathed with my cousins in summertime,
Rowed in my grandfather's coracle, or ever
Slept with my head on the afternoon arm
Of Mourne. Not, not once have I made
The pilgrimage along the Drogheda Road
Where, crossed with stone, stands the martyrdom
Of James O'Hanlon, who died at the hand
Of the Black and Sin, the Blood and Tan.

From Ireland exiled in the womb, still,
Like the birthmark of the mother's wild
Craving at labour, that stamps the child,
I wore the shape of Ireland on my mind.
I can brush Lake Sligo when I take
The tear from my eye, or when I talk
Hear the foiled tongues of the streams
That cannot convert rocks to their water

Near Mornington. Not mythological dreams
I am haunted by, Ireland as my daughter;
But by the wild obscurity of Leinster, by
The giant shore of the West, greater than heroes:
By the tongue of the Boyne in my ear, and by
My cousin's letters, more than myths or stories.

Having no nearer Hesperides, I create
Ireland my Hesperides near at hand—
No more the sentimental cloud land
Of cuckoos and kisses than national hate
Creates more sea in the Irish Channel. No,
I mean my own Ireland which no latitude
Can categorize and no map show—
Because only I possess the plenitude
Of passion it has—only I know
The lonely inhabitant, whose home is
Imagination. Nothing of Ireland I know,
Except that the point from which grew
My sentimental pearl, is Ireland to you.

Prohibited sentimental pleasure,
Like the sadist I revert to the real.
Here's Europe's sore that will not heal,
Struck by a sword to gain a seizure.
Although people move gaily in the streets,
Daft with drink or mere God's breath—
Cottages rot and men eat roots,
Dogs starve at doors, towns close, and Death—
Death the bookmaker takes most of the proceeds.
Not to be laid, the spectres of Collins,
Swift and Connolly, Mac Swiney Mayor of Cork,
Mourn like statues that sweat and bleed,
Watching Ireland at her usual work:
Weeping among the seed potatoes.

Elegy on Spain

Dedication to the photograph of a child killed in an air-raid on Barcelona

O ecstatic is this head of five-year joy—
Captured its butterfly rapture on a paper:
And not the rupture of the right eye may
Make any less this prettier than a picture.
O now, my minor moon, dead as meat
Slapped on a negative plate, I hold
The crime of the bloody time in my hand.

Light, light with that lunar death our fate;
Make more dazzling with your agony's gold
The death that lays us all in the sand.
Gaze with that gutted eye on our endeavour
To be the human brute, not the brute human:
And if I feel your gaze upon me ever,
I'll wear the robe of blood that love illumines.

I.

The hero's red flag is laid across his eyes,
Lies by the Madrid rock and baptizes sand
Grander than god with the blood of his best, and
Estramadura is blazing in his fallen hand.
All of a fallen man is what is heaven's;
Grievance is lowered to a half-mast of sorrow,
Tomorrow has no hand in the beat of his breath, and after
Laughter his heart is hollow.

For a star is against him, that fallen on his forehead,
Forward is blocked by the augury of our evil.
Sin is a star that has fallen on our own heads.
Sheds us a shower of chlorine, the devil's revel;
Evil lifts a hand and the heads of flowers fall—
The pall of the hero who by the Ebro bleeding
Feeds with his blood the stones that rise and call,
Tall as any man, 'No pasaran!'

Can the bird cry any other word on the branch
That blanches at the bomb's red wink and roar,
Or the tall daffodil, trodden under the wheel of war,
But spring up again in the Spring for will not stay under?
Thunder and Mussolini cannot forbid to sing and spring
The bird with a word of determination, or a blossom of hope,
Heard in a dream, or blooming down Time's slope.

But now for a moment which shall always be a monument
Draw like a murder the red rag across those eyes.
Skies in July not drier than they are,
Bare of a tear now that pain, like a crystal memorial,
Is their memorials scattered over the face of Spain.
Together this hero and the ghost of the Easter Irish,
Brother and sister, beaten by the fist of the beast,
Water tomorrow with the tears and blood of slaughter.

II.

Go down, my red bull, proud as a hero,
Nero is done with, but the Hungerford Hundred,
The Tolpuddle Martyr, the human hero,
Rises and remains, not in loss sundered;
Plundered, is proud of his plenitude of prizes.
Now spiked with false friendship, bright with blood,
Stood did my bull in the pool of his passion,
Flashing his sickle horn as he sinks at the knees.

Peace is not angels blessing blood with a kiss;—
Is the axis pinning Spain through the breast
To the water-wheel that makes a nation a martyr
To the traitor who wheels the whips of gold and steel.
O bold bull in the ring, old ox at the wheel,
Sold for a song on the lips of a Hitler,
No halter shall hold you down to the bloody altar
Longer than life takes to rise again from slaughter.

This flower Freedom needs blood at the roots,
Its shoots spring from your wounds, and the bomb
Booming among the ruins of your houses, arouses

Generation and generation from the grave
To slave at your side for future liberation.
Those who die with five stars in their hands
Hand on their ghosts to guard a yard of land
From the boot of the landlord and the band of war.

Drop, drop that heavy head, my less and more than dead,
Bled dry a moment, tomorrow will raise that hand
From the sad sand, less than death a defeat.
Beaten by friend, not enemy, betrayed, not beaten,
Laid let that head be, low, my bull, stunned,
Gunned from the royal box by a trigger pull.
Bigger no courage is than the blood it can spill.

Not in a wreath I write the death in a ring,
But sing a breath taken by heroes, a respite:
No fight is over when Satan still straddles a man;
Then the real battle begins which only ends
When friends shake hands over the break of evil.
O level out the outrageous crags of hate
To those great valleys where our love can slant
Like light at morning that restores the plant!

O Asturian with a burst breast like an aster,
Disaster sports blooms like that in many places;
Graces the grave of a nation with human pain.
Spain like a sleeping beauty finds her kiss
Is the lips of your wounds awakening her again
To claim her freedom from the enclosing chain.
Silence the blackbird, take away the tree,
He will not need them until he is free.

At evening is red the sky over us all.
Shall our fiery funeral not raise tomorrow also?
So shall the order of love from death's disorder
Broader than Russia arise and bring in the day.
Sleep gives us dreams that the morning dissolves,
But borne on death we reach the bourne of dreams.
Seems blood too bitter a bargain to pay for that day?
Too bitter a bargain, or too far a day?

Draw then the red sky over his eyes, and Sleep
Keep Orion silent above him, and no wind move
Love's leaves covering him at the French border.
The marauder snuffles among his guts for a night:
Right is capsized: but Spain shall not drown,
For grown to a giantess overnight arises,
Blazes like morning Venus on a bleeding sea,
She, he, shall stretch her limbs in liberty.

III.

Madrid, like a live eye in the Iberian mask,
Asks help from heaven and receives a bomb:
Doom makes the night her eyelid, but at dawn
Drawn is the screen from the bull's-eye capital.
She gazes at the Junker angels in the sky
Passionately and pitifully. Die
The death of the dog, O Capital City, still
Sirius shall spring up from the kill.

Farewell for a day my phœnix who leaves ashes
Flashing on the Guernica tree and Guadalajara range.
Change is the ringing of all bells of evil,
Good is a constant that now lies in your keeping
Sleeping in the cemeteries of the fallen, who,
True as a circling star will soon return
Burning the dark with five tails of anger.

What is there not in the air any longer,
Stronger than songs or roses, and greater
Than those who create it, a nation
Manhandling god for its freedom? lost,
O my ghost, the first fall, but not lost
The will to liberty which shall have liberty
At the long last.

So close a moment that long open eye,
Fly the flag low, and fold over those hands
Cramped to a gun: gather the child's remains
Staining the wall and cluttering the drains;

Troop down the red to the black and the brown;
Go homeward with tears to water the ground.
All this builds a bigger plinth for glory,
Story on story, on which triumph shall be found.

To David Gascoyne

The marble Caesar who weeps his face away
There in the royal gardens by the royal river
Where in the summer
We talking walked the mazes of small dreams—
This Caesar now steps down into our day,
Striped like a sabre-tooth with blood and anger,
Warsaw a fig in his jaw, death as his drummer,
Messerschmidts on his lips and in the dark
Buoy of his eye the knowledge of his crimes
Beating a seabell.

Nevertheless we shall walk and talk in the park
With a bird's verve over the pell mell,
Celebrating the human perennial and the
Sexual ecstasy of dialectics, marrying impossibles,
From whose bridal bed, the dovetailed fury,
God's born again.

What can we do at the crux of acts but sleep
Ambered in visions, hung in the illstarred hammock
Kissing the wounds of miracles? Let me keep
Warm the hole in the breast from which I bleed,
Remembering this was struck by the hand of hope
Whose fallen angel face gnaws at my stomach
Riddling me with illusion. Now I shall remember
The Tudor Gardens, the girl-pleasing fountains,
The torn postcards in the lily ponds,
And I shall speak of love on every first of September.

Letter to a Friend

What have I waited for the third of my life
Any more than you have waited for, a great grave?
When I have heard the blue-eyed bird on the wave
Trumpeting his courage over a sea of grief
Keeping his cage and kingdom above the water,
I wondered why not lay that wing low, lay
That wing low, and lay that crest on the wave—
Rest, rest, my fine fellow, for death is easy.
But he blows from his beak and braves the wave.

O feathery friend, I have found a friend
Who tells me of a place where I shall find
A feather heavy on my mouth and never mind.
I shall lie quiet, sleeping above the wind.
O feathery friend with a flame in your hand
Fighting for life in a fog of sorrow,
Give up the ghost that shudders in the marrow,
Leave the cage empty on the rotting strand;
I know where today is as easy as tomorrow.

The weals where the whips stripped me at my shoulder
Heal up and on my back I bear festoons of flowers;
The cut is lips where I drink peace and power,
And love, instead of growing older and colder
Squanders its smile in a Cheshire grin; the smile
The horizon has, meeting the vague of space.
And there I lie, not remembering even
The times I crashed my head against heaven,
Not remembering even a friend's face.

Can I coerce you, O my fine feathery friend,
Across the Andes and the world's siren fields
Where women mourn for me before I come
And dream of love with me when I am gone?
Ecstatic world where you and I have kissed
Touching in love's lucky tangent, now
I veer off like the banking plane, and below

Glimpse the last shimmer of your wing in mist.
O Ecstatic world where we met, but might have missed!

I have a haven I carry in my hand—
Death like a regicide poison in my pouch,
Rendering me happy with its least touch.
I have the heavenly key of a knife in my hand.
I have a friend who at my worse need
Will aid me with a blade stuck in my back,
Giving me the kiss of death indeed.
He is my friend who comes at the fatal beckoning
And opens up the great gates of the dead.

O my fine friend, I have a gift to give,
A pinch of dope to ease all your trouble.
I carry death as surely as all alive,
Contagious, incredible, acting at the double.
When I have given you flowers and tokens,
How happily the petty things you've taken—
I have a better gift to give you now.
What have you waited for the third of life,
But the end of a life's grief?

When you were lost, what were you looking for?
Or when you were absent, what was it from?
Now you are lost, and looking for your home.
Now you are absent from the peace of no more.
Let me, my fine gay one, take you to my place,
The great gap of absence where no one is:
Let us lie down on the edge of that lake,
Thinking a moment all that this poem is.
Then we will go together into the whole of this.

And when we wait a while on the verge,
Taking a glance behind at the gay, going things,
Giving our goodbye to all rememberings,
Then, as one disrobes of clothes, we shall slip the urge,
The bloody ache of being and going on being;
Loose off the rags of flesh and mask of whom;
The watch, the revolver, and the mirror of second being:

Revert again to the air of the Mary womb,
And not feel the weight of the open tomb.

O feathery friend with a fiend in your hand,
Scotch him before he wears you to a tear;
The great tear that lives because it quivers,
The pearl of sorrow from his point of sand.
Give up the ghost that all men fear,
The spirit of life that gives meat the shivers.
O my fine feathery friend, give me your hand—
I am the ghost of a ghost that was never here.
I know the place for those without lives.

Pacific Sonnets

I.

Between the wall of China and my heart
O exile is. Remembering the tremendous
Autumnals of nations threatening to end us all,
I speak of the things nearest to my heart.
These space cannot alienate, or time part
From me: O is it really an end of them,
The flowering moments that a poem blends
To Babylonian wreaths around my heart?

The arguments under arches in the rain
With lightning in our fists, the summer drives
Through the Dorset hills, evenings at the baths
With echoes exploding like bubbles as we dive
Down to quiet worlds: these, if not again
To be our happy lives, shall be our happy death.

II.

Those whom I may not meet pester me now
Like dogs I lost seem leaping at my breast,

But lost, lost across space, found in a daydream
Only, or foundered in the floundering west
Go under whispering messages that blow
Over the world and pester me with home.

And O more lonely than the only John
Who found his paradise on a minor island,
I sit among the hands and faces that mop and mow
Among the smothering mountains of my silence
Like lizards of reminiscence flashing recollection
They glitter at me from crags and peaks
And my heart begs that one of them speaks,
The evanescent faces that pester me now.

III.

And in these islands hung in the fringe of Asia,
The herbaceous border of the Siberian waste,
Where I move giddily in disgust or aphasia
Straddling the huts of paper and paste,
Here in this vacuum where goldfish float
Between transparent planes of mental negation
But look like thoughts, here on this glass
I see reflected the mechanism of fate
Evolving the instruments of destruction
For all that I have left, the Europe that was,
Whose historical frieze, in its seizure,
Shrieks with the voice of Sibelius, crying
Like a violin in the middle of the sea,
'I am dying!'

IV.

By the now westward China, and, to the east
The spoiling, coiling, the blue beast toiling sea,
All my thinking is how circumvented,
And sleep that takes me home again is best.
Not the September typhoon or earthquake indented
Shore, the cholera epidemic or the war,
Punishes my nights with such violence
Or crushes my days between such a wall and sea:

So much as absence whispers in the evening
The sentimental commitments that I've broken,
And the images I've known and the words I've spoken
O crush me between them where they grieve
Like clouds. So that all my thinking is
Circumvented by memory and a kiss.

[*Three Memorial Sonnets for two young seamen lost overboard in a storm in Mid-Pacific, January,* 1940.]

V.

The seagull, spreadeagled, splayed on the wind,
Span backwards shrieking, belly facing upward,
Fled backward with a gimlet in its heart
To see the two youths swimming hand in hand
Through green eternity. O swept overboard
Not could the thirty-foot jaws them part,
Or the flouncing skirts that swept them over
Separate what death pronounced was love.

I saw them, the hand flapping like a flag,
And another like a dolphin with a child
Supporting him. Was I the shape of Jesus
When to me hopeward their eyeballs swivelled,
Saw I was standing in the stance of vague
Horror; paralysed with mere pity's peace?

VI.

From thorax of storms the voices of verbs
Shall call to me without sound, like the silence
Round which cyclones rage, to nurse my nerve
And hang my heart midway, where the balance
Meets. I taste sea swilling in my bowels
As I sit shivering in the swing of waves
Like a face in a bubble. As the hull heaves
I and my ghost tread water over hell.

The greedy bitch with sailors in her guts
Green as a dream and formidable as God,
Spitting at stars, gnawing at shores, mad randy,
Riots with us on her abdomen and puts
Eternity in our cabins, pitches our pod
To the mouth of the death for which no one is ready.

VII.

At midday they looked up and saw their death
Standing up overhead as loud as thunder
As white as angels and as broad as God:
Then, then the shock, the last gasp of breath
As grazing the bulwark they swept over and under,
All the green arms around them that load
Their eyes their ears their stomachs with eternals,
Whirled away in a white pool to the stern.

But the most possible of all miracles
Is that the useless tear that did not fall
From the corner of their eyes, was the prize,
The flowers, the gifts, the crystal sepulchre,
The funeral contribution and memorial,
The perfect and nonexistent obsequies.

VIII.

Hawaiian aerodromes, the Pekin Summer Palace,
Cyclonic Kamchatka, the yellow archipelago,
Laokoon China and the circles of snow,
I look among them for the herbs of solace
To soothe an absence, or to find a place
Where among the amazing masks and the gingko,
The seismics, the diseases, the natural disasters,
I can clear a space for my own past.

But always the riverside willows tease
My eyes to tears; the message-crisscrossed sea
Goes mocking backwards and forwards but not for me,
And the huge clippers, skimming the parallels,

Their language of birds, taking the wrong course,
Tell me nothing but what a silence tells.

IX.

So in a one man Europe I sit here
Thinking a peace and a perfect map
Also for the epileptic hemisphere.
What now obsesses us all is shape
Whose horrible mutations, like a birth,
Shed more blood than they're worth,
Like idiot sons. The shape of hope
Is nevertheless innumerable and rises
From all the postures and the disguises
Of loss and defeat and even Europe.

But whistling in the dark brings images
Back that were for a moment on a furlough,
And so my dark is full of mirages
And voices make a birdcage of my pillow.

X.

It's flowers and curtains for my Chrysostoms.
My golden mouths go dumb in these paper rooms
Without foundations, stuck around vacuums:
This is the place where all negations cross.
Catastrophe without tragedy, agony without passion,
No love at all but sex by the session,
Action by reflex without human compulsion:
Here history is events without a cause.

O the horses of torsion that tear life apart,
Or the hooks I hung on, the engines of agony,
Devolve our primogeniture upon us the far
Side of existence, and we sweat our glory.
Tragedy is our mother of the pearl, and her
Heart is our lachrymatory and laboratory.

XI.

Thus when our torso melts on the grate
We can hear happiness whistling in the distance
Or in another room, at a future date
Calling us with the cicada's persistence
To another place and another time
Where in a summer's country under dimmer
But kinder constellations we can find
Godetia peace sprouting from the hammer.

So the bloody needle of hope in my chest
Goes nosing over months and latitudes
To what home of a moment where I shall lie
At rest among the things I like best.
Thus the apes of life, riding the back with rods,
Jockey us towards impossibles but why.

XII.

And now there is nothing left to celebrate
But the individual death in a ditch or a plane
Like a cock o' the north in a hurricane.
Out of the bogus glory and the synthetic hate,
The welter of nations and the speeches, O step down
You corpse in the gold and blue, out of a cloud,
My dragonfly, step down into your own:
The ditch and the dislocated wings and the cold
Kiss of the not to be monumental stone.

This is the only dignity left, the single
Death without purpose and without understanding
Like birds boys drop with catapults. Not comprehending
Denudes us of the personal aim and angle,
And so we are perfect sacrifice to nothing.

XIII.

Everywhere is our wilderness everywhere.
I hear the scapegoat's scream wherever I go

And not only from my throat but also
Everyone is our scapegoat everyone.

When by the ilex I lie in the sun
Thinking I'm free for a moment, then the crown
Of bleeding christian leaves comes down,
The scapegoat coronation also there.

Or in a world of palm and anthropoid
The shape of Darwin gibbering descends
Out of the leaves of life and from a void
Condemns me to a beginning and an end.
Thus everywhere is our wilderness everywhere,
And everyone is our scapegoat everyone.

XIV.

Goodbye then the island colonised by ideograms,
Of poverty and moongazing, hate and gardens,
Where the soul is shallower than a bowl of tea
And negative as water. And goodbye also
The opposite island of Gothic paradigms
Whom history too heavily burdens,—
Goodbye my white home in a lachrymose sea,
Too wise to be true, too stupid to be false.

Goodbye the stone angels and plush chairs,
The solicitor's plates worn to anonymity,
The parks where the duke's deer wander, the spring
A national resurrection, the lawyers, the liars:
Goodbye equally my kind and consanguinity,
Now all that is left is always everything.

Secular Elegies

I.

My pig-faced kingdom with tongues of wrong
And an historical gait of trial and error,
Under whose bridges Time, faster than rivers,
Bears individual and event along
Into a past overloaded with souvenirs:

Now answer history with a marvellous golden Yes
As she steps up asking all future questions.
The historians in their tombs, sighing, will sleep
Deeper, and the sailors, who always had great visions,
Smile for the island that ceased to be an illusion.

The instinct of the bird governs its acts of war,
Who, titivating itself at crossroads, rises and rises
Singing from the destructive wheels that come roar-
ing towards it, and in the end, after the reverses,
Perches whistling on the shattered axles proudly.

The armies of Hohenzollern, brooding on loss,
Know best that the real enemy is never there
Pinned akimbo on the gun-sight, but in the cause.
O sheeted in their horoscopes like togas
Under red stars strut the catchpenny Caesars.

Heroes who ride your wishing horses over
The breakfast tables of the population,
Your beds are full of hands. And when you shiver
What stalks across your grave is a whole nation:
And when you close an eye your life is over.

But the conquerors, reddening their heels on us,
They will not ever really die, but continually
Thrash on the hotbed of their animus:
Not one of them shall die hopefully and finally,
For them the grave will also be full of us.

II.

Where formerly he saw birds in bushes, now
The cyclist resting from his uphill labour
Observes the skull of Cromwell on a bough
Admonishing his half heart, and he shoulders
His way upward against the wind to the brow.

The political cartoonist in his bed
Hears voices break his sleep he does not know:
The morning papers show what the people said.
Librarians in their studies, the lights low,
Sense Milton breathing in his marble head.

The clerk hears Clive cheering in a darkness.
And from the ponds of commons, in broad day,
The effigies of great sailors rise in their starkness
With the *Hood* in their hands, and cry:
'Nevertheless we mourn also the *Bismarck*!'

There it is necessary to walk carefully
And swallows must dive wisely, for the air,
So full of poems and ghosts, is truly
Populated with more than meets the eye:
Some principles have become poltergeist there.

Where, in its sepulchres, the long past rests
Brocaded with daydreams, there the truth is known:
What makes the people happiest is best.
But the fish in its undersea caves and bird in its nest
Know that the shark and cuckoo never rest.

Sometimes the punts in summer on the rivers,
Gliding like dancers over the slovenly water
Saw as they traced their way among the shallows
Images under them pinned in a cage of shadows
Struggling to catch the eye. It was the future.

The quavering Chamberlain, trapped between disasters,
Hiding his head in an hour-glass: four kings and

The bicyclist Queen, like uprooted pilasters,
Flying across the sea: coiled in the ampersand
The hakencreutz accumulates but never masters.

And some, in silence, looking for their lives
In the lines of their hands, the merciless words saw
That turned Nebuchadnezzar into a cow:
Others, who came kissing and bringing olives,
Had a change of heart and are dead now.

Sad in his alcove of love Pascal lamented:
'My friend, my friend, you were born on the other side.'
Firstly we die because of places. O the demented
Alexander, who, eternally discontented,
Desires more, is us. Finally we die of pride.

III.

Satan is on your tongue, sweet singer, with
Your eye on the income and the encomium:
Angels rhapsodise for and from their faith.
And in the studies of chromium
Lucifer seduces Orpheus with a myth.

But the principle of evil is not autonomous.
Like the Liberty Horse with a plume at a circus
Under the whipmaster it steps proud in its circles.
When I let slip one instant the whip of the will
All hell's scot free with fire at the nostril.

Thus if the crux and judgement never is
Left to our own to do with as we will,
But the decision, like a master key, lies
Wholly in the higher hands that hold all—
How can we be as innocent as this?

Everything that is profound loves the mask,
Said the Dionysian who never wore one.
Thus our damnation and our condemnation,

Wiser than Nietzsche, never taking a risk,
Wears the mask of a necessary satisfaction.

Not, Love, when we kiss do the archangels weep
For we are naked then wherever we are,
Like tigers in the night; but in our sleep
The masks go down, and the beast is bare:
It is not Love but double damnation there.

Marooned on the islands of pride, lonely
And mad on the pyramids of achievement,
Disillusioned in the cathedrals of doxology,
The sad man senses his continual bereavement:
God has just died, and now there is only

Us. The gold bull with its horns of finances
Over the sensual mountains goes gallivanting
In glory: all night and all day it dances,
Absurd and happy because nothing is wanting.
The sad man hides his grief in his five senses.

IV.

Then from its labours I rest my hand on the table
And there where hitherto the poem had been,
Now, in its deadliness sleeping but capable,
Agent and gadget of destruction, the machine
Of actual damnation lies and is culpable.

Everything that we touch, sooner or later,—
The uprooted arbutus hung at the head of the bed,
The untouchable trophies in the arcanum of nature,
The dizzy stars, the testes, and the sacred
Dove—everything that we dissect for data
Dies as we finger for the heart of the matter.

O but the Doric arm tattooed with falsity
That riddles this embrace where worlds hide,
Larger than railways where they hold a country

Sleeping and waking in their iron anatomy,
Takes me to the breast where I am pacified

Under the frenzies of all sensual wonders.
What shall I say when, big at my mouth,
The Hesperidean with a worm in its splendours
Hangs like the bub of a whore? Or what truth
Find in the kiss that dazzles all my windows?

And so in circles over existential deserts
I and you wander, lost, and arm in arm;
Lost, lost. And the visions paying us visits
Lead us to mirages where, in a morning dream,
We forget the headaches and the lost Edens.

V.

O Golden Fleece she is where she lies tonight
Trammelled in her sheets like midsummer on a bed,
Kisses like moths flitter over her bright
Mouth, and, as she turns her head,
All space moves over to give her beauty room.

Where her hand, like a bird on the branch of her arm,
Droops its wings over the bedside as she sleeps,
There the air perpetually stays warm
Since, nested, her hand rested there. And she keeps
Under her green thumb life like a growing poem.

My nine-tiered tigress in the cage of sex
I feed with meat that you tear from my side
Crowning your nine months with the paradox:
The love that kisses with a homicide
In robes of red generation resurrects.

The bride who rides the hymenæal waterfall
Spawning all possibles in her pools of surplus,
Whom the train rapes going into a tunnel,
The imperial multiplicator nothing can nonplus:
My mother Nature is the origin of it all.

At Pharaoh's Feast and in the family cupboard,
Gay corpse, bright skeleton, and the fly in amber,
She sits with her laws like antlers from her forehead
Enmeshing everyone, with flowers and thunder
Adorning the head that destiny never worried.

VI.

Temper the whirlwind to the unborn lamb,
Mother of us all, lapped in your shawls of cause;
Large in your arms wrap our sad amalgam
That, spinning its tails among the other stars,
Mopes, lost and weeping, far, far from its home.

Cover with your pity the broken Pole
Where, like a rag, the pride of the human hangs
Dirty as dishcloths. And with summer console
Us for the equinox of our anguish.
Humour the arrogant ships that sail.

Too near the tooth of the truth and the weather,
The thinkers in their cockleshells, the captains
Sinking each other; and always permit neither
Wholly to find their ends, for they seek islands
Of Death and Truth that should always be further.

And in due season to their last bed take
The lovers who are the cause of all the trouble;
Let the manikin Adam successfully undertake
What Atlas only, bending an apish double,
Hitherto managed with the world on his back.

O temper the whirlwind to the unborn lamb!
And on the tongue of the young in its cradle
Lightly lay silver spoons. And the same
Love extend to those who groom your bridal
That they, mother of us all, suffer in your name.

Sacred Elegies

ELEGY I

I.

From this window where the North Atlantic
Takes the crow in my mind home in a short line
Over the kissing fish in the wave, and the mine
Where the sailor clasps his death as mermaid like
Sex of a knife in the bed, from this window
Watching I see the farewelling seasons fall
Ever between us like rain. And the lachrymal
Memory, trailing its skirts, walks like a widow
Across those seas looking for home. O the Dido
Heart! Sail, sail the ships ever away from us all.

II.

Then at this midnight as instant as the bell
That bangs the sailor from his bed to Europe,
I see tomorrow grow in a tree of hope
Outside the window where, like a branch with a ball,
Your face of kisses hangs in my love
Shattered and happy. The sixteen winds that blow
The small seeds into each other's arms below,
The birds to their boughs above, the sad and evil
Everywhere, shall bring to you, if nothing else avail,
The love that, never coming, always goes.

III.

To cross the divide and desert of this distance
Only a hand is enough. Like the seamew sweeping
The wave with a wing to rise up weeping
The parted heart shall with a bird's persistence
Cross seven oceans to its proper home. The pigeon
With a hundred hieroglyphics at its claw
Less laden drops down with what's waited for
Than the sea-weary home-comer returning. O let love imagine

Meetings of the long parted at the door
Of expectation with smiles in the margin.

IV.

Lovers for whom the world is always absent
Move in their lonely union like twin stars
Twining bright destinies around their cause:
They dazzle to shadow with a meridian present
The wallflower world. Redundant it shall resent
The kiss that annihilates and the gaze that razes.
O from their clasp a new astronomy rises
Where, morning and evening, the dominant Venus
Dismisses all sad worlds that turn between us,
And we shall kiss behind our mask of faces.

ELEGY II

I.

Peace for explorers who come late upon water
I call the kiss of the foot on its native stone
After the separation of seas and the strange zone.
The madmen wandering across wildernesses, later
Look up and see the palatial womb and the home.
The maternal mirage lifts up its arms and says, 'Come'.
Cold under bridges a stranger freezes. The lost
Tankers heading their sad cortege in from the North
Not knowing which hemisphere gave them birth,
Shall sigh up their smoke sinking at last to rest.

II.

Speak, then, of peace where the white child lies quiet
Sleeping in shadows between privation and pain:
Where the pink daughter drops back to bed again
After the visitor in the sheets, and red as riot
My father rises and condemns society.
Let me speak of peace among the proletariat

Protesting against life with a flag and a slogan,
Resigned to the empty gesture and the empty
Belly. Speak, then, of peace before death began
Foreclosing on the not yet buried man.

III.

The Decalogue is written on their sheets
Where, watching life through windows, (the fish
Flying in wind, tattering trees with wishes,)
Exiled from existence, the invalids, like secrets,
Inhabit amber rooms. Only the dream completes
The landscape of that odd island where they dwell
With the two-headed child and the ghost. Their lives
File past the foot of the bed like negatives.
O the castaways in bedrooms! Exiled they shall
See Patmos visions exalting all that survives.

IV.

Far from his home he dies in beds or deserts
With all the necessary angels at his head,
The lover in fever and poverty. The remembered
Image of Love comes down and, hushing his hurts,
Folds him in wide arms and takes him home to that dream
For which he is always seeking. The maternal
Mirage emerges in tremors of eternal
Concern. 'Come to the womb, come, for it is home.'
O invalids in love and indigence, return
To the hands of stars and the universal bosom!

ELEGY III

I.

The laurelled skull spoke from St. Helena:
'Cold kingdom. Huddled in cloaks of pride on peaks
The giant egoists freeze among the wrecks
Of conscience and custom. Caesar has been

Set snarling at large in the ethical arena.
All law is down. The giant egoists, mad
As engine drivers from responsibility
Mow down their Roehms in the insensibility
Of pride gone beserk and vanity gone bad.'
Alone on the altitudes alive and dead.

II.

The conscious supermen, grinning in style,
Wearing elected parliaments in their lapels,
Gaze out of newspapers at all those peoples
Who fight and believe and die under their smile.
Sacred in crystal Stalin shall sleep and
Be illegally illustrious. But at his foot
The dachshund and the private diamond lie.
Somewhere an Austrian corporal shall be mute
At whose word once, from Europe to the sky,
Suddenly everyone everywhere began to die.

III.

The colossal Apollo. The sky-writer with
Guilt in his thumbmark, the poet with the human
Hanging at hand, cut with a verb to the nerve,
Rabbits at butchers. The arrogant wreath
Bright at his face, the Mephistophelean omen,
Both wards away and draws a man and woman.
O seeking at all altars a Sybilline to serve
Either in beds or wars, he finds only
The anthropoid I gibbering from mirrors. Lonely
The poet walks among a score of selves.

IV.

Akimbo on mountains the heroic egoist
With poems or murders or empires in his pocket
May also remember Love. Sometimes a dove has kissed,
And, leaving a lock of conscience in a locket,
Haunted him with memories of the human. Then,

Then from his loneliness will rise up sorrowing
The spectre of what is lost; the common growing
That gives the grass its ergatocratic green.
The solitary heroes. Who shall take them in?
Glittering they shiver on the rocks of knowing.

V.

And we, scissored at birth from the past,
Step down out of genealogical tapestry,
Where, shoving shoulders with example, we
Rubbed elbows with great precedents. At last
Liberated independent we are lost,
The scapegoat generations. The patriarch on his column
Gazes out on our dilemma in stone.
What hand can he extend across the schism
Breaking between us in years? But on our own,
Clasping a spirit we walk water home.

ELEGY IV.

I.

Evolving under the architrave of their love
The lovers, intertwining like doves on a doorknocker,
Sometimes have joined. And, meeting above,
Like the springing swords at a military wedding,
The kiss is consummation. From an ark of isolation
The beasts of love emerge in pairs and bring
Hymenæals here. Antitheses meet and look deep
Into each other's eyes at Love's dictation.
And on their happy bed in a summer evening
The Lovers answer Lucretius in their sleep.

II.

But who at the kiss, who has not seen, over
The waterfalling hair at the shoulder of Life,
Death from his own face staring out of a glass?

Some shall be most alone with a lover, never
Letting the sweating hand unlock that closet of
The coffined I. O sometimes, nevertheless,
The labourer at his instrument or tractor,
Bending into a state of merge with objects,
Finds the same love that, from a machine of sex,
Steps down as Venus to her invoker.

III.

Labouring, the lover shall become that Apollo
Who in a Spanish square stared at a dog
Till it gave up the ghost and ran off empty.
Not alone then, the poet shall know temporary
Wedding with all things: in divine divorce less
Suffer the alienations of that loneliness
When, for an instant, awakened in the dark,
The marital poem, with bouquet and catalogue,
Tenders her gifts on his bed of the oligarch.
He shall be joined for an hour with a dog.

IV.

Thanatos, thanatos! The labourer, dropping his lever,
Hides a black letter close to his heart and goes,
Thanatos, thanatos, home for the day and for ever.
Crying, from the conch of Venus the emergent Eros
Breaks free, bursts from the heart of the lover,
And, at last liberated from the individual,
The solitary confinement of an evil lease,
Returns to the perfect. Azrael, Azrael,
Enters with papers of pardon releasing
The idiot poet from a biological cell.

ELEGY V

I.

These errors loved no less than the saint loves arrows
Repeat, Love has left the world. He is not here.

O God, like Love revealing yourself in absence
So that, though farther than stars, like Love that sorrows
In separation, the desire in the heart of hearts
To come home to you makes you most manifest.
The booming zero spins as his halo where
Ashes of pride on all the tongues of sense
Crown us with negatives. O deal us in our deserts
The crumb of falling vanity. It is eucharist.

II.

Everyone walking everywhere goes in a glow
Of geometrical progression, all meteors, in praise-
Hosannas on the tongues of the dumb shall raise
Roads for the gangs in chains to return to
God. They go hugging the traumas like halleluias
To the bodies that earn this beatitude. The Seven
Seas they crowd like the great sailing clippers,
Those homing migrants that, with their swallow-like sails set,
Swayed forward along the loneliness that opposed,
For nothing more than a meeting in heaven.

III.

Therefore all things, in all three tenses,
Alone like the statue in an alcove of love,
Moving in obedient machinery, sleeping
Happy in impossible achievements, keeping
Close to each other, because the night is dark;
The great man dreaming on the stones of circumstances,
The small wringing hands because rocks will not move:
The beast in its red kingdom, the star in its arc:
O all things, therefore, in shapes or in senses,
Know that they exist in the kiss of his Love.

IV.

Incubus. Anæsthetist with glory in a bag,
Foreman with a sweatbox and a whip. Asphyxiator
Of the ecstatic. Sergeant with a grudge
Against the lost lovers in the park of creation,

Fiend behind the fiend behind the fiend behind the
Friend. Mastodon with mastery, monster with an ache
At the tooth of the ego, the dead drunk judge:
Wheresoever Thou art our agony will find Thee
Enthroned on the darkest altar of our heartbreak
Perfect. Beast, brute, bastard. O dog my God!

First Cycle of Love Poems

I.

This morning take a holiday from unhappiness because
It is the greatest day there ever was
When he stepped down out of the nuptial arch
With the cross in his face and he shall search
For ever for the wreath and not even at his death
Really regret this day that gave him birth.

O history be kind and time be short to him
Where he is anonymous and let him come to no harm
From the hammer of the diurnal, or the drum,
The sweatbox and the wheel where the dog's dream
Turns and is interminable. O be near always
You whom from far I shall not the less praise!

Let the gentle solstice, like the Fierral Bay
Where the Eleven Thousand Virgins keep
The fishes quiet in their arms, keep him asleep
All his life long in a long summer's day:
With the empty hourglass, the four-leafed clover,
The rock for the resurrection, and much love.

II.

Here at my hand here at my heart lie still.
Will then the prince of index finger, your caduceus,
Alight on my lip like a dove on a window sill
Delivering in its claw the symbolic oleaster?

Here at my heart here at my hand lie still
Till the dog-rose springs off its beds of bush
To run in circles leaping at your heel,
And nature, happy, curls up at your kiss.

Lie still, lie still, here at my heart lie still
Sleeping like thunderheads. Be over me dominant
So I shall sleep as the river sleeps under the hill
Kissing the foot and giving back the element.

Here at my hand lie still; lie still at my heart.
Sesame is on his tongue and the unicorn rages
Round the abdominal amphitheatre. I hear
His double engines drumming up the passages

O till his cumulus, over the angry bed
Arching, is rainbows. Volplane my bomber
Shuttling silver through the night I bride;
He spins his disc of kisses in my slumber.

And I lie still in heart and hand lie still,
All the streamers of welcome flaunting in my marrow
And flares I lift my arms are, because he will
Come down descending on my bed like a meadow.

Then here in my heart he lies as dark as pillage
Where in my arms I hold
The murderer who, Samsoning up my five pillars,
Lies quiet now, for here at my heart I fold him.

III.

The kiss is maypole where my seven
Happiest sins truss me to the rod:
The lightning cracks my face of heaven
When he leans down, when he leans down like a diver
Out of his breast's cloud.
The flammenwerfer and the fish
And also I acknowledge him creator.

Between his horizon of arms measures my wish,
My mirage of marriage that, one moment later,
Comes true in a flash.

O at your work you patient hundred thousand
With the hammer, the hour and the pen,
His harder labour is love. He has emblazoned
Everything, overnight everything's blossomed
With Love again.

IV.

Then like the ship at rest in the bay
  I drop my sails and come home
To harbour in his arms and stay
  For ever harboured from harm.

On his foot's beach my combers ride
  The vaulted coral where he stands,
And spray against his rock of side
  Showers that fill his hands.

O whirlwind catching up the sea
  And folding islands in its shawls,
Give him to me, give him to me,
  And I will wrap him in my shallows.

O the Red Sea parted long ago
  When the angel went whistling through,
My seas rise up in pride also
  To let his chariots through.

The masculine cliff-face gazes out
  At the smile of the horizon,
And disregards the sea that flaunts
  Her beauties by the dozen.

So he looks out over my subjugation
  Where the combers coil at his feet,
And sees, the far side of adulation,

My Hesperides rise singing, one moment, from the ocean,
   And the next, sinking, weep.

But from the altitude of hid domination
   O sometimes, like waterfalls,
His hand comes down through a gravity of anticipation
   And a constellation of nuptials.

Nightly to his archipelagoes where
   Apples adorn the pillar,
My kiss of fishes moves in schools and bears
   The body to him on a silver platter.

The syzygies, over our Balkan bed,
   Shed silver on the peninsula,
Against whose shores my waters beat their head
   Like rain on a red star.

The narwhal with a spike on its brow
   Spins thrashing through the wave:
His love is mine, who lashes now
   In the sweat of seas I gave.

Then morning, like a monument
   Glittering in a tree,
Reminds me of a former moment
When the first star was immanent
And the mountain, dominant,
   Leaned down and kissed me.

V.

My joy, my jockey, my Gabriel
Who bares his horns above my sleep
Is sleeping now. And I shall keep him
In valley and on pinnacle
And marvellous in my tabernacle.

My peace is where his shoulder holds
My clouds among his skies of face;

His plenty is my peace, my peace:
And like a serpent by a boulder
His shade I rest in glory coiled.

Time will divide us, and the sea
Wring its wild hands all day between;
The autumn bring a change of scene.
But always and for ever he
At night will sleep and keep by me.

Second Cycle of Love Poems

I.

By the lake where we walked in the summer,
  There where our bed was,
Now the sad cedar sheds our remembered image
  Like autumn on the grass.

And the rainclouds, giving suck to the mountain
  Above the lake, foretell
What in anticipation I recognized
  Was yours in parallel.

II.

O tender under her right breast
  Sleep at the waterfall
My daughter, my daughter, and be at rest
  As I at her left shall.

At night the pigeon in the eaves
  Leaves open its bright eye;
Nor will the Seven Sisters cease
  To watch you where you lie.

The pine like a father over your bed
  Will bend down from above

To lay in duty at your head
   The candles of its love.

And in their mothering embrace,
   Sleep on the Rockies' bosom;
The Okanegan Valley shall grace
   Canada round your cradle.
The silver spoon and the one-eyed man,
   The rabbit's foot and the clover,
Be at your bed, from morning till
   As now, the day is over.

III.

My dragonfly roaring your engines
   Through my five senses soar,
As, seeking for its origin,
   The bird goes up through the shower.

And over all that distance can
   Or time will put between us,
Rise O my rainbow and make span
   Over what intervenes.

On their cotillion axles spin
   The automatic stars,
And take our silver kisses in
   Like penny pianolas.

But far from me as my home is
   You move, and do not rest,
With tang at your tongue my thousand-mile kiss,
   And the babe at the breast.

IV.

And in your hand, with tears for water,
   Proving what I cannot prove,
The myrtle springs up out of the stigmata
   As martyrs spring from Love.

So from the guilt, O my capital,
  What rises, what rises,
But the pillar of atonement, crowned
  With roses, with roses.

V.

By those shallows where once Sorrow was
  No one now moves, for everyone is absence
  Holding my heart in their empty hands, as
Squalid with loss, I am remembrances.

Shatter what waters. Your eyes bitter with
  Obituaries like blinds. All Time is over
  For ever, and for ever the memory in a wreath
Marks our separation on the shattered water.

Come home the masturbators in the gasmasks,
  Bloated with rubber kisses and homicidal
  Embraces. Whatever the disaster asks
I give it, heart and all. O happy suicidal!

The eagle kills me. Sing, birds and bombers, sing!
  Spangled with spinners, rising, pulverising,
  Roaring up angles where Love like a scarecrow dangles,
Crissed on the crosses because existence is wrong.

Colder than drift the kiss is at parting,
  The smarting bliss in the lifted hand, and Always
  Written in a gesture. The air goes colder.
Rise O you angels with engines at the shoulder!

My place is under and further and not here—
  The candle disappearing in the thunder.
  Never to find, not here, not anywhere,
The sleeping bed where I curl in a hand.

VI. [Verses for an Anniversary]

To you who at my side with sweet water
Always have stood in the summer,

And in the bitter season and the storm
With breast and kiss have kept me warm,
I give the permanent element,
The poem in the acknowledgement.

To you whom neither penury nor the crucial word
For which I barter bed and board,
Could ever divide, as, at my side,
You stood in humility and pride,
To you I render what is little enough
Of prizes but I give all my love.

And for the losses, the tears, the errors,
The holidays I took in mirrors,
The snowball debts of the self-denials
You piled upon me, for these I also,
Seeking with words somehow to defray,
Acknowledge it is impossible ever to pay.

VII. [Verses for a First Birthday]

Hang at my hand as I write now
My small one whom the dogs follow,
That, nuzzled in my stomach, dance
Like sea-lions with her innocence.

The roaring forties in the bed
Beat up disaster on her head,
And on the wall the calendar
Always enumerated War.

Thunder in the teacup and
Prognostications in the sand
Menaced her amusements with
The abracadabra of death.

She who kisses prettier than
Two breezes meeting round a fan,
What shall she hold in her arms
But the catastrophes like lambs?

And when, among the temporal
Ruins of her landscape shall
The giddygoat and Cupid chase
All but Disney from the place?

On the rag of a single summer
She dried all the tears of the future;
The vernal equinox was up her sleeve
When the winter made her grieve.

Happily the unhappy shall lie down
By her, and bounty be her own
Bubble: the hitherto inconsolable
Find solace at her first syllable.

The dove, in its code of coos,
Will carry abroad her good news:
That it was Love, and not
Laws kept the Ark afloat.

For the desire, and the daughter,
And the dog chasing its tail,
Renew all things in Nature,
And Nature renews it all.

VIII.

Leaning in the evenings, I live
  Between a dream and a mask;
The dogs of memory, howling, shall
  Mourn on the steps of the heart.

Lost in the temporal labyrinth
  How shall I find that exit?
O follow backward the fallen face and the fragments
  Of desecrated existence!

Then everywhere I shall discover
  In a mnemonic room

The spectre in a glass sepulchre
With a child on its arm.

From the small tree calls to me
The voice of the devoted
Turtle dove, that, forsaken in the myrtle,
Utters the last of love.

'I wish you anguish and wild seas,
Cataclysms and thunder,
So that in extremity you long for me
And the bed of my gender.

'The forked lightning, kicking
Its gold legs across the sky,
Tell you how once, between my knees
Fighting, you rose to die.'

The swan at midnight hangs its head
Singing, into my mirror;
And in the morning, by my bed,
Lies still beside its fellow.

Then everywhere I discover
In a mnemonic room
The spectre in a glass sepulchre
With a child on its arm.

Third Cycle of Love Poems

I.

This is that month, Elizabeth,
When at the equinox
Biological life divests its death
Equating the paradox
That crosses its dovetails underneath
All internecine sex.

Where silent once, where silent once
   Bedded in negatives we
Held hands across the Winter whence
   This April lets us free,
Now up, now up in the solstice dance
   We join with biology.

Generation towards generation stirs
   Of human and animal.
Prime causes, giving birth to stars
   Give equally to all
The multiplications of universe
   In animal and amoeba.

This is that day, Elizabeth,
   When the lamb and the child fed
From your horn-plentied hand as both
   Begged you for love and food.
The cuckoo, recalling in aftermath
   When he was your performer,
Remember shall in Winter with
   Double delight this Summer.

Shattering wreaths all spectres rise
   Taking their first deep breath:
The seas go gadding with bright eyes,
The dead gods get up and rejoice
   At circumventing death:
And to all these I join my voice
   In Love, Elizabeth.

II.

Where the kissing systems turn
   Arm in arm across the sky
And the sleepless years return
Red-eyed, haunted, to their high
   Stations in astronomy:

There, shaking water at parallax,
   Lolling along distances,

The morning lets the stars relax
And makes a magic among tenses:
   Love rises from her bed of senses.

The systems, wheeling in degrees,
   Speak in eternal vocables:
'The heart, through all its allegories,
Shall always walk the stellar alleys
   Clasping an astrolabe of troubles.'

Thus, crosswise on antinomies,
   The angel and the anthropoid,
The wrongs and the responsibilities
   Making love across a void
   Kiss in a shower of pities.

III.

Shut the Seven Seas against us,
   Lock the five continents,
Set sepulchred the North Star
   In a forsaken tense:
Lay every Sun and System
   For ever in a dark bed,
Nevertheless that day shall dawn
   That resurrects the dead.

When sleepless the wakes, weeping,
   Mourn life under every leaf,
And the Moon covers her eye over
   Rather than look on our grief,
When in their dreams the liars and
   The loveless regret life,—
Then, then the dove born in every storm
   Shall arrive bright with olive.

Step, Primavera, from your bed,
   Dazzling with existence.
Put the Sun and the Moon and the Systems right,
   Hang heaven on circumstance.

Lean from all windows like waterfalls,
  Look, Love, on us below,—
And so from their somnolence in sense
  All things shall rise to you.

IV.

The village coddled in the valley,
The bird cuddled in the cloud,
The small fish nested, the babe breasted,
Sleep with a deeper dream endowed:
For them this evening especially
Hangs its veils over all the world.

Whickering child and weeping lamb
Interchange in the general care
That Nature, cradling kind in her arm,
Extends to all new things that are:
As, walking clouds, she keeps from harm
The whickering child and weeping lamb.

Fourth Cycle of Love Poems

I.

My tall dead wives with knives in their breasts
Gaze at me, I am guilty, as they roll
    Like derelicts in my tempests,
Baring their innocence to the dirty pole
Whirled upon which I am a world at rest.

But restless in the bed of the will of things
I sleep with knives: the wave overhead
    Shall kiss with fangs
Red with the lipstick of their dead love
Above me as I lie in the grave of a bed.

O sex of crystal, foretell expiation
That like a feather, lightly, upon a father

Fall shall from the pain of the immolation:
    Then let me gather
Nothing but vipers to my satisfactions.

Like women of windows all red in morning
My wives walk down roads in rags and tears.
I know where they go and with what meaning.
    Everywhere is their
Wide and wilderness world beyond redeeming.

II.

Then to question all things
  That suffer and do not die,
I also go down all roads and
  Ask everything why.

The anguish in the darkness, or
  The sobbing in the roof,
The tears in the tree will not
  Assuage my grief.

And the still day sits
  With its face of cancer,
Nor will the silent hour
  Give me an answer.

III.

The denominations and the categories,
  The primogenitures, the powers,
How can they alleviate their histories
  Since we must suffer ours?

When I move my hand to unlock the
  Birdcage of her eyes,
I hear, beating on political bars,
  The demigorgons of policies.

At evening when her dark face is laid
  Against the light of kiss,

Then the shadows of a red decade
  Obliterate all brightness.

Thus Justice, with the world in one hand,
  And lovers in the other,
Observes all life dying in its divisions,
  But regrets nothing.

IV.

Less the dog begged to die in the sky
  Immortal and transfixed,
Or the tall tree to grow on ground
  Later axed and annexed,

Than my dark one, my sweet stark one,
  Begged the knife in the breast,
The long lie, the lying worm in the bed,
  The cheat I attest.

But bull without a bell I trod
  Among her mysteries,
Simpleton with a bomb I hid
  Shivering in her caves;
And her hand came down out of a cloud,
  Her beauty from the shadows
Emerged and suffered what I did
  To mitigate my sorrows.

V.

I nailed on wood by her eyes
  Shall feel her tears start
From my hands and feet; so my lies
  Stick vinegar in her throat.

All my maternals she is. And she is
  Eternal to forgive
The snake of love striking at her caress
  Invidious to survive.

This one means to me what the sea
   Means to the fish and bubble,
The arms around me, the lullaby,
   The rockabye of trouble.

Through the tunnels of our conjugals
   Her flutes and my bugles blew,
So Time, from walking, waltzes towards
   New joys that renew.

The double conundrum of our one
   Breaking in two to be,
Gives me her daughter and gives her
   My son in Gemini.

. . . . . .

Love, that invests us with evil,
   With retribution now
Rectify wrongs and level me
   With salt and plough.

The colts, all legs, go gallivanting,
   Between a sire and dam,
But a week of sea and war bangs between
   Them and where I am.

The ache at the break of the heart
   Is nothing: a pearl knows this.
What remains eternally intolerable is always
   The justice, the justice.

VI.

When we look angels in the face
We smirk and gibber to the rear;
When the moon rises with our tears
Smiles make a sunset of our gaze.

The spitting bitch shall lie down and
Breed beds of cherubs; the weltering whale
Shelter all Jonahs from the gale;
The overproud shall understand.

The twins at the head and foot of the bed
Smiling and weeping, bright and dark,
Shall keystone kiss a dialectic arch
To let our oppositions wed.

VII.

At this white window by the Thames
Where swans elide the labials of water,
I sit and I must speak those names
That, since my tongue is swan on thought,
Are brought to my mind by these themes.

Here I span stones at twelve, and under
Bridges rigged bonfires with ragamuffins
To warm a wind that chased us. O send a
Kinder wind to them, the bigger urchins,
And wherever they are now, Time, be tender!

No, names that mean nothing, not
To a verse I give you, idle recompense,
Not to hereafter show you, but
Now as I sit gazing at your absence,
I sense the gang of you hanging about.

'Bugger,' I hear a whisper, 'the door's locked.'
'They're coming, they're coming, they're coming,' cries
The ginger one that luck liked.
'O my God,' my adolescence sighs,
'I could have seen it if I had only looked!'

What are they made of, these images
Of recollection calling me in the evening,
Memorialising the irresponsible stages?
And why are they continually intervening?
What shall I answer to their messages?

Though long gone, a war and world ago,
Nevertheless they remain, bobbing and banging
At the dust-shuttered reminiscent window

Where I now lean—ghosts whose hanging
Hereabouts makes me a memory also.

Joe, you down mines, may see me when
The lens of sweat glistering at the eye
Shows all the past in a crystal. Then
See you me moving as formerly
I moved near you and never shall again?

No, they go sadly or proudly about
The business of their being, with
No wasted sentiment, and without
Skeletons inhabiting their faith.
Shall I spend what they will not?

Because, anonymous and simple,
They grow, like leaves, on the big tree
Where, on a twig, I try my trumpet,
They are the consummation of the
Existence that is their example.

If, singing their praises, I raise
A word that, by their virtues, lasts
Half as long as they deserve,
Then these hobnobbers of my past
Shall live as long as ever.

VIII.

My love who sleeps lost in America
Dreams distance gone, then I am at her side
Where she lies smiling, because no longer
Lonely we sleep as the wide seas divide.

Nightly, O nightly, hovering lightly over
This moment of meeting between chronologies,
Star in the dark, far in the mid-Atlantic,
Our two loves, like doves, meet in their kiss.

Personal Sonnets

To My Mother

Most near, most dear, most loved and most far,
Under the window where I often found her
Sitting as huge as Asia, seismic with laughter,
Gin and chicken helpless in her Irish hand,
Irresistible as Rabelais, but most tender for
The lame dogs and hurt birds that surround her,—
She is a procession no one can follow after
But be like a little dog following a brass band.

She will not glance up at the bomber, or condescend
To drop her gin and scuttle to a cellar,
But lean on the mahogany table like a mountain
Whom only faith can move, and so I send
O all my faith, and all my love to tell her
That she will move from mourning into morning.

To My Brother

And you, my shy one with a pin in your eye
Where I fixed half a blindness, my brother,
You as gentle as water and simple as oxygen,
Shunning the compromise and the clever shadows,
Now, like a singing sheep dragged out to die,
Sing, sing up out of the fiery abattoir:
And only to hear your voice your voice again
I'll come down to join you in the sorrows.

No, let not this one, O let not this one
Clutching the tooth of Hitler in his chest
See the red spittle of my own blood ooze
Between his fingers: for this one is one
Whom wombs cannot restore, or time redress,
Nor I or the whole world recover if we lose.

To David Gill

Or you, new father of a blonde daughter, born
Between a gutted Warsaw and an Oslo sold,
With your knee-riding son, and nose for weather,
Subscriber to liberal papers and the Sailors' Fund,
The monument of the tremendous normal,—
Where are you now, not wandering on the wold
Between Godalming and the sea-blossoming heather,
Or spitting half-crowns in the village pond:

But mad as a mechanic with a broken spanner
Stand pointing an empty rifle at the East;
Or, like the Spring embedded in November,
Lie hoping for resurrection in Stavanger
Under the stone and snow. Yes, now you rest,
With so many ordinary things to remember.

To Stephen Spender

This poet with his soul upon his shoulder
Trudging up a world's steps to bring to those
Who shiver by the embers of their optimism
The hundredweight of his pity, now to him
I wave a word as the times grow colder
And our tears freeze to giant stars and close
The eye of love with death's bleeding prism.
Will war make blind, vision wrong could not dim?

Let me see now not the irregular fountain
Whence poems rose like crystals, glittering truth,
But the tall chap with a leg like a flying buttress,
A hand for a saw or bow, a face worth a fortune
But for the distorted torture of the mouth
Which to his words of truth bore such a witness.

To T. S. Eliot

Expecting a bomb or angel through the roof,
Cold as a saint in Canterbury Cathedral,
This gentleman with Adam on his mind
Sits writing verses on cats that speak: lives
By the prolonged accident of divine proof,
A living martyr to the biological.
Hell spreads its horrors on his window blind
And fills his room with interrogatives.

St. Thomas doubting and not doubting,
Confident of God, but dubious of human,
I render my tongue merely as minor flame
To glorify this inglorious martyrdom:
And when the bomb or angel breaks the vaulting
Trust he remembers, among the others, my name.

To Any Member of My Generation

What was it you remember—the summer mornings
Down by the river at Richmond with a girl,
And as you kissed, clumsy in bathing costumes,
History guffawed in a rosebush. O what a warning—
If only we had known, if only we had known!
And when you looked in mirrors was this meaning
Plain as the pain in the centre of a pearl?
Horrible tomorrow in Teutonic postures
Making absurd the past we cannot disown?

Whenever we kissed we cocked the future's rifles
And from our wild-oat words, like dragon's teeth,
Death underfoot now arises; when we were gay
Dancing together in what we hoped was life,
Who was it in our arms but the whores of death
Whom we have found in our beds today, today?

Sestina at 34

I have come down half the overcrowded avenue
O Rhadamanthus, you to whose kingdom I journey
With seven children and several books on my shoulders
All screaming. I have left wounds on some pavements
So that your dogs and furies, hounding the heart to a stone,
Know where I go and where I have left my handmark.

I do not know the purpose of this journey
Between the big breasts and the grounded shoulders
Save that, in some way, by scribbling on pavements,
The man glorifies both himself and the godlike stone.
O morning strike bright along this flashing handmark
I scrawl across Time in its heavenly avenue!

When my love groans with babies and books on its shoulders
This is the proud load of the labouring pavement
Ascending into the sun to burnish a stone.
Christopher, you would know. Saint, set your handmark
On my child-ridden forehead. Water this avenue
With the sweat of an infant-carrier on his journey.

Heavy my heart walks ahead on the pavements
With her high-heel shoe my martyrdom on stone:
Everywhere the red heart lies is a landmark;
I am in the right road, the slaughterer's avenue.
Mother of all things, Love, approve my journey
With a fair share of lightning on my shoulders.

I am at midday. Bells rage in the stone
Arch of the chest. The sky wears my handmark
Where I have held it. Summer the avenue
Here where Alighieri started a hotter journey,
Summer more suffering, manhood beating the shoulders,
Than any winter or April. And on the pavements

Fate, photographer, fixing, in shadow, his handwork;
Recording, for ever, in image along the avenue

The lies and the lives we lived. This is a journey
Dollied by the unsleeping eye. No head and shoulders
Shunning the sinning loin, but, naked as pavements,
Every step stopped a monument in stone.

Avenue of myrtles and births! Lovers like statues
Unmoving in evening, all Eden on a pavement!
O journey of hazard and heroes, monster and blizzard,
Who happy unhappy as I when I slip from my shoulders
The heavy bag of the ego, and, dead cat by the pavement,
Lie down under my God's immemorial stone?

Summer Song I

I looked into my heart to write
  And found a desert there.
But when I looked again I heard
Howling and proud in every word
  The hyena despair.

Great summer sun, great summer sun,
  All loss burns in trophies;
And in the cold sheet of the sky
Lifelong the fishlipped lovers lie
  Kissing catastrophes.

O loving garden where I lay
  When under the breasted tree
My son stood up behind my eyes
And groaned: Remember that the price
  Is vinegar for me.

Great summer sun, great summer sun,
  Turn back to the designer:
I would not be the one to start
The breaking day and the breaking heart
  For all the grief in China.

My one, my one, my only love,
   Hide, hide your face in a leaf,
And let the hot tear falling burn
The stupid heart that will not learn
   The everywhere of grief.

Great summer sun, great summer sun,
   Turn back to the never-never
Cloud-cuckoo, happy, far-off land
Where all the love is true love, and
   True love goes on for ever.

Summer Song II

Soft is the collied night, and cool
These regions where the dreamers rule,
As Summer, in her rose and robe,
Astride the horses of the globe,
Drags, fighting, from the midnight sky,
The mushroom at whose glance we die.

The Five Faces of Pity

1.

The gift of the spirit that destroys man's reason
O real supernatural friend, let visit me now.
I have seen the vision lie down with the illusion.

O real supernatural friend, teach me how
To bear witness in this darkness to those graces
Whom, glory folded about them, I cannot know.

War, the unbearable beast in the sky, effaces
These effigies of Pity that rise up on a cloud:
The living and the dying hide their faces.

Dragon in nebulae. Death has endowed
Each of us with a cockeyed crown of remorse.
We walk in a world where even the flesh is proud.

Sigh, O you far stars, weep over the whole universe
Where, grieving, the great blind is drawn and the one
Solitary crow circles silently over our house.

Will the labours of Pity never be done?

2.

On a war's bed I was watching beside water:
Saw through a window Pity asleep on the quiet
Lake like a figure afloat on the eye of Nature.

Sleeping her swan had, in the stormcentre of riot,
Calmed fury like that onetime walker on waves
Who so amazed the water with his spirit

That it obeyed. For all creation behaves
As it is told by our impassioned faith.
Division exists only to prove who loves.

Then I saw Pity get up like a wraith
And step in sleep about her cosmic hovel:
Where her foot fell atonement laid its wreath.

But the loud ineffectual uproar of our evil
Crowds silent space. The immortal mirage
Flies off, in light, on its eternal travail

Till all space shimmers with our immoral image.

3.

May it not, somehow, become fatal for all those
Who have solicited the various adverse powers
To advance them in an unforgivable purpose.

May mercy alight on the lionlike's last hours
When he wrestles among enemies; and may rain
Quell the sick seas of every heart that suffers.

Let the hero die happy knowing he died in vain
Glory. To the drowned man and dying infant allow
One dazzling instant when the truth is plain.

Comfort always the cause. Fill its responsible pillow
With an absolution of sleep. Lead the somnambulist
To the restless bed of desire that he follows.

Return to the logician the seven stars of mystery
Without one missing, the crucial star of Pity:
And, commemorating forever the occasion when they kissed

Let the Nations live on the crossed world in amity.

4.

To those who have established their habitations
On the edge of the wilderness, the outcast and the pariah;
To those for whom life is an exercise in patience

The invalids; and to those who continually aspire
After lost satisfactions and vanished destinations,
The self-flagellant ambitious; to those who require

Visions of evidence in measurable dimensions,
An angel with a yardstick to testify of glory;
To the fanatics who set fire to hospitable conventions;

To the proud on their ostriches riding down history;
To the innocent soldier killing; to those whom no
Wind of mercy can cool to the conciliatory;

To the blunt-headed violent who do not know
How many births and deaths any action involves;
Finally to all of us who are culpable here below—

O Woman of Pity, extend the love that absolves.

5.

My love for my love kills my mind, my master:
My love is my master, my love is my mind:
My love is divine, and Pity is his sister.

Where my love walks Pity shall always find
Many for her administrations continually appealing;
Where any love walks my victims are dragged behind.

Love fills the universe with victories more appalling
Than avalanche, volcano, or all war. Its rule
Tyrannicidal. These purposes transcend appraisal.

But when, like War, love walks over the whole
World and leaves it wrecked in a wilderness
From this excess of passion, who, who shall console us?

Where my love walks Pity shall redress
All the world's wrongs. Walking at night outdoors
The cosmological ruins whisper as I pass:

What Love destroys, Pity always restores.

Ode Against St Cecilia's Day

Rise, underground sleepers, rise from the grave
  Under a broken hearted sky
And hear the swansinging nightmares grieve
  For this deserted anniversary
Where, horned, a hope sobs in the wilderness
  By the thunderbolt of the day.

Footfall echoing down the long ruin of midnight
  Knock like a heart in a box
Through the aural house and the sibylline skull
  Where once Cecilia shook her singing veils,

Echo and mourn. Footstepping word, attend her
  Where, here, bird of answer, she prevails.

Sleep, wormeaten weepers. Silence is her altar.
  To the drum of the head, muffled
In a dark time, the sigh is a hecatomb.
  Tender Cecilia silence. Silence is tender
As never a voice was. Here, dumb-
Struck she mourns in the catacomb of her grandeur.

O stop the calling killer in the skull
  Like beasts we turn toward!
For was the nightriding siren beautiful
Caterwauling War until her bed was full
  Of the uxorious dead?

Let the great moaners of the seven seas
  Let only the seas mourn,
With the shipwrecked harp of creation on their knees
  Till Cecilia turns to a stone.

News of the World I

Cold shuttered loveless star, skulker in clouds,
  Streetwalker of the sky,
Where can you hide? No one will take you in.
Happy the morning lights up other worlds
As from sleep they turn a family of faces
To the houseproud sun. Outraged, you, outcast,
Leading your one-eyed sister through the night,
From door to door down the locked zodiac,
  Never come home.

News of the World II

In the first year of the last disgrace
  Peace, turning her face away,
Coughing in laurelled fires, weeping,
  Drags out from her hatcheted heart
  The sunset axe of the day.

And leaning up against the red sky
  She mourns over evening cities:
The milky morning springs from her mothering breast
  Half choked with happy memories
  And fulfilment of miseries.

'I am the wife of the workman world
  With an apron full of children—
And happy, happy any hovel was
  With my helping hand under his gifted head
  And for my sleep his shoulder.

'I wish that the crestfallen stars would fall
  Out of his drunken eye and strike
My children cold. I wish the big sea
  Would pity them, and pity me,
  And smother us all alike.

'Bitter sun, bitter sun, put out your lions
  As I have put out my hope.
For he will take them in his clever hand
And teach them how to dismember love
  Just as though it was Europe.

'O washing-board Time, my hands are sore
  And the backs of the angels ache.
For the redhanded husband has abandoned me
To drag his coat in front of his pride,
  And I know my heart will break.'

In the first year of the last disgrace
   Peace, turning her face away,
Coughing in fire and laurels, weeping,
   Bared again her butchered heart
   To the sunrise axe of the day.

News of the World III

Let her lie naked here, my hand resting
Light on her broken breast, the sleeping world
Given into our far from careful keeping,
Terrestrial daughter of a disaster of waters
No master honours. Let her lie tonight
Attended by those visions of bright swords
That never defended but ended life.
My emerald trembler, my sky skipping scullion,
See, now, your sister, dipping into the horizon,
Leaves us in darkness; you, nude, and I
Seeking to loose what the day retrieves,
An immoderation of love. Bend your arm
Under my generation of heads. The seas enfold
My sleepless eye and save it weeping
For the dishonoured star. I hear your grave
Nocturnal lamentation, where, abandoned, far,
You, like Arabia in her tent, mourn through an evening
Of wildernesses. O what are you grieving for?
From the tiara'd palaces of the Andes
And the last Asiatic terraces, I see
The wringing of the hands of all of the world,
I hear your long lingering of disillusion.
Favour the viper, heaven, with one vision
That it may see what is lost. The crime is blended
With the time and the cause. But at your
Guilty and golden bosom, O daughter of laws,
I happy lie tonight, the fingering zephyr
Light and unlikely as a kiss. The shades creep
Out of their holes and graves for a last

Long look at your bare empire as it rolls
Its derelict glory away into darkness. Turn, liar,
Back. Our fate is in your face. Whom do you love
But those whom you doom to the happy disgrace
Of adoring you with degradations? I garb my wife,
The wide world of a bride, in devastations.
She has curled up in my hand, and, like a moth,
Died a legend of splendour along the line of my life.
But the congregation of clouds paces in dolour
Over my head and her never barren belly
Where we lie, summered, together, a world and I.
Her birdflecked hair, sunsetting the weather,
Feathers my eye, she shakes an ear-ring sky,
And her hand of a country trembles against me.
The glittering nightriders gambol through
A zodiac of symbols above our love
Promising, O my star-crossed, death and disasters.
But I want breath for nothing but your possession
Now, now, this summer midnight, before the dawn
Shakes its bright gun in the sky, before
The serried battalions of lies and organizations of hate
Entirely encompass us, buried; before the wolf and friend
Render us enemies. Before all this,
Lie one night in my arms and give me peace.

Turn on your side and bear the day to me

Turn on your side and bear the day to me
Beloved, sceptre-struck, immured
In the glass wall of sleep. Slowly
Uncloud the borealis of your eye
And show your iceberg secrets, your midnight prizes
To the green-eyed world and to me. Sin
Coils upward into thin air when you awaken
And again morning announces amnesty over
The serpent-kingdomed bed. Your mother
Watched with as dove an eye the unforgiveable night

Sigh backward into innocence when you
Set a bright monument in her amorous sea.
Look down, Undine, on the trident that struck
Sons from the rock of vanity. Turn in the world
Sceptre-struck, spellbound, beloved,
Turn in the world and bear the day to me.

The Bridal Nightmare I

Nightmare in whose arctic wings
  Lifelong I unmoving lie
Folded at your cold heart I sleep
  Outside in uncharity.
Bridal nightmare, sheeted, stained,
Broken, now, is that vain idol
Bespoken bridegroom I beside.
That cracked cup, an empty heart
Fell away and, from my hand,
Slipped lie and poison on my pillow,
Lie lifelong here at my left side,
Unspeaking and unspoken bride
For every side we lie beside
Satifies and is satisfied.
Unbridled nightmare, day bedfellow,
I am my nightmare, awake, asleep;
Creep out, creep out, cold man, and comfort
  The wrongs where they weep!

The Bridal Nightmare II

Who locked you in the shuddering
  Rock that will rot and die
The day that you turn your suffering
  Face away?

Who fixed you in the form
  From which, ghost in a wall,
You look out on the workings of a will that
  Forgives us all?

Who pinned you on a crossroad where
  With bright limbs spread
It is you who are glittering like a star and
  We who are dead?

I established you in the diamond of
  The undiscoverable heart
All dazzle hidden. How can such brightness not
  Inspire the dark?

I with a hand of guilt laid stone
  On rock to cover you over,
Only to find that I had made a shade
  Matter for ever.

The kiss is diagonals on which you die
  Smiling in sweat because
The turn of your face away would undo
  The cross of a kiss.

Who rubs our double destruction together
  Save procreative fate,
So that we shed the fire, the child, each other?
  Turn, turn away your face!

The Bridal Nightmare III

By what I walk the curse of my lifted eye
  Peoples with memory
Clasping and kissing as bright snakes in shadows
  Hiss the wicked story
And the apple is struck and resounds like a gong

In the cuts of the misery
So that no side can smother and no mother hide
The groan of the purgatory
Babe in the pride of the abandoned bride.
I have died beside the cursed and lifted
Heart where an ego cried out,
Out! I have walked by the bereft
And I was left alone
Cuddling the cold stone of a green-eyed ego:
I watched you and the lamb go by
Cold in the curse of my eye
Or run to the butchering gun of my hand
As I lifted the axe of abandoned
Love over you and lamb, love over you and lamb;
Till the crime sobbed in the womb
And, swaddled in time, stepped down the red-boned thigh
Into a worse world. The rockabye
Cradle ticks like a clock in my breast
And the judgements build up in the west
Where, like a sun, I labouring without rest,
Die night by night. Bright shawl
Of the morning, cover the bones of all those
By whose lost hearts I fall,
And over the bleeding sea of my dereliction cast
Darkness at last.

To my Son

Part I

My darkling child the stars have obeyed
In your deliverance and laid
You cold on the doorstep of a house
Where few are happy and times get worse.
I will not gild your nativity
With a desirable lie, nor pity
The birth that invests me with a second
Heart on which I had not reckoned:
No less than I do you will drink

Cold comfort at a loveless brink,
And when the wheel of mischance grazes
You as you play I shall know pauses
Of the skipping heart. Let the day, bending
A bright hand about you, attend you
Into the fatherless night when we
Are each of us alone and at sea
Without a North Star—but may
The night seem safer the next day.
The best of all is not to be born,
But how can we tell this to the morning
That, as we groan, comes up over the hill
Of our midnight grief? I see you, still,
An unbroken daybreak in my darkest
Heart, destined to illuminate the stark
Day of necessity in proper season.
Why were you born? I love. This is the reason.
But do not ask me why or whom—
Does it much matter what prefix doom
Wears to her name? She and I
Shall always meet when all wishes
Under a dazzle of unpropitious
But irresistible ascendencies
Clasp each other because they freeze.
I saw her face. Saw fate had taught her
That she was an elected daughter
And in obedience to the pull
Of that which knows it is beautiful
I moved towards her in the cold
And fell into a moon. The golden
Undergrowth of her sex enmeshed
The dying fugitive it refreshed
For henceforward daily dying.
Sucking blood a Venus, sighing,
Toys her prey back into life:
He rules her with the sexual knife
That kills him. But all this
Comes later, my dear son, and is
Knowledge of a kind that seems
Too bitter for the simple schemes

Of a world in which the killer
Neither hates nor loves the killed.
Your bed is a kingdom where
Tears pacify the dogs of despair
And the cold sheets, getting warm,
Protect you all night long from harm.
My bed is made. I lie on love
Like dynamos. The rub and shove
Turn generations on their way.
We weep as we embrace and die.
When the normal day begins
We, rising, step out of our sins
Not even smiling. The monsters settle
Back into their sleeping metal.
My dear son, you rode down on
The spinal throes of a mastodon
One quiet night in May. I bare
That hour because I do not dare
Let flesh grow over it. Your own
Heartburst, one day, like a cyst,
Will fester so, if you desist
From speech. The tongue is a bird
Where the worm, in the heart interred,
Can be caught by no other. Let him, ringing
Lark of the bloodiest field, bring
The overworn heart relief. I write
These lines in a train on a night
You sleep away in Ireland. Do not stir.
I would not have my unpleasanter
Thoughts disturb you. It is late.
The moon stares down, dispassionate
As the world stares up at her.
All things are lost in genera.
The train crawls on. The coast creeps near.
The rain has started. And the year
Is almost ended. I have been
Too long away from my domain:
Too much pursued my own will o'
The whips against a stranger pillow,
Too many seas of wounds sailed over

To think that destinations cover
The running sore of separation.
I, like the train, must learn my station
And stop a while there. Let me hide
My restlessness at your bedside,
Where, my dear son, you keep
Four better guardians of your sleep.

Part II

Will those, my son, who love us most
Ever, this sad side of the ghost,
Be satisfied that they ask
Enough of us? The Augean task
Faces everyone who is able
To sit down at a loving table:
Just as the ice-hearted stars
Stand around like avatars
Knowing that every cosmic crime
Will come again in its good time.
And I have seen, with bloodshot eyes,
Across the domesticities
Mopping on a farther region
The visage of the demogorgon.
O heavy-handed seraph, smooth
The lying pillow with a truth:
The coiling sheet of kisses stirs
On liars in their sepulchres.
Rise, babe, and gibber on the cross
Where dissimulation was,
Until in its proper season
A skull steps from the Hill of Venus.
My son, I delegate you all
The trophies of the temporal
If I give to you a heart
In which the human has no part;
But since, my dear son, you breathe,
Hop your own skip. Underneath
The human heart, I believe,
Lives a god who cannot grieve

No matter how disastrous
The crimes our passion brings on us
Because this ungrieving god
Knows that either bad or good
Might look, from a better angle,
Like a double-headed angel.
Nevertheless, how can we,
Victims of crashed astrology,
We, O how can we look down
And see the heart that was our own
Guzzled, with whimpers, by the bitch
Because she loves? And of us, which
One never, in the street, like dogs,
Mounted Desire? O pedagogues,
You can teach that Justice is
Exacted on us, but to us
It is what we do, because
We remember what innocence was.
I shall not ever here again
Watch your sleep, my dear son,
With the whole raindrop of the sky
Covered up in your bright eye,
And every sweet beast of creation
Standing around in its station
Because the child and animals
Know nothing of these enigmas,
The seven hymning orthodox
Damnations on the bloody rocks:
Know nothing, sweet son and green lamb,
Of the satanic 'I am'
That opens up a rock of wrath
And shows us the golden path
To that glass palace where Love
Keeps her prize pigs. Let me leave
Now, as evening's eyelashes
Hide the day's scar as it flashes
And the lions of the sunset die
Among the wires of the sky,
Let me leave, now, these cold lines
Which your Father also signs.

Sonnet of Fishes

Bright drips the morning from its trophied nets
Looped along a sky flickering fish and wing,
Cobbles like salmon crowd up waterfalling
Streets where life dies thrashing as the sea forgets,
True widow, what she has lost; and, ravished, lets
The knuckledustered sun shake bullying
A fist of glory over her. Every thing,
Even the sly night, gives up its lunar secrets.

And I with pilchards cold in my pocket make
Red-eyed a way to the bed. But in my blood
Crying I hear, still, the leap of the silver diver
Caught in four cords after his fatal strake:
And then, the immense imminence not understood,
Death, in a dark, in a deep, in a dream, for ever.

Sonnet on Ireland

Remember, Dev, the vision in Sackville Street
Who shoved a gun in your fist and cried out loudly:
'Justice, Justice!' Remember how proudly
The longhaired talkers died on their hanging feet
So that blindfolded woman might turn her head
Just for one last look at them? Did it assuage
Their living or their dying when her image
Burned through the rag because such men were dead?

That was an Eire ago. Did she die
With the mackintoshed generals of her liberation
Strung up at a lamppost in the English dark?
She traipses the backstreet of Ireland unseen by
Any Taoiseach. She keeps assignation
With the shade of Connolly chained in Phoenix Park.

To Yankel Adler

There was that Jew making love to a chair
What did it do? O avatar of Love
It turned back first of all into a tree
Then to the seed, then to the hand that planted.
He ran his brush down the back and laid bare
The hundred thousand hearts of the objective.
He handled a wooden leg and physiology
Gave up a tabernacle. This is what he wanted.
Eavesdropper on the gossiping of sorrows
How do you never frighten them? They stay
Exchanging those secrets, like birds, in your presence
For which I count the feathers of my sparrows
But overhear nothing. Then why do all things obey
Your hylic hand? It is because you are absence.

To Charles Baudelaire

Walk with me, Sir, when nothing perpends
The wilderness within me. When I adhere
To the trumped up altar because I fear
An obscure answer, see that your ghost attends
Me, for what reason? Knowing I do not deserve
Vision or vigil of your serpent spirit
Untwined from knowledge to make me that visit,
Nevertheless I entreat. I serve
Much the same master. Was your good a god?
I hate my ruler because he will not break me
Under the overloving justice of his rod,
Thus but for love I hate him. Take me
To that inverted golgotha you trod
And, O Sir, show me the mirror that will break me!

To Father Gerard Manley Hopkins, S.J.

Overhead on a wing under heaven, treading
   Bright verbs on silence, writing red on hereafter,
He is for ever his feathers of sunset shedding,
   Bedding all beautiful in the far harder and softer
Breath of his word, bird in a thrash alighting
   All claws for the world that his heart is after,
The wide wonder that, into his talon of writing,
   Rose up, eyes open, to meet her emasculate master.

Father of further sons who wear your plumage
   For the good glory of the word, I speak for
All of us who inherit any merit of your image:
O long-faced convert, look down and seek for
   Worthiness in one of us, and let him speak
   Evangelizing the incomprehensible message.

Sonnets of the Triple-headed Manichee

I.

I was with that man when he rummaged his hand
Among the guts of a god to fish for doves:
The true wound chides that side without a wound
For tendering nothing that attests or proves
What telltale vision sleeps in a red hand.
O from the wild and green hole of the human
Heartful of lies and the forked tongue of grief,
Let now the hooking claw of my doubt summon
The glittering colossus of disbelief.
I pitch through those receding zeroes of
The doubt that, like recurring sevens, riddles
The sum of all things. We are crucified
Like serpents of the intellect on circles—
O wounds, O crowns, O zeroes, bleed at my side!

II.

Keelhauled across the starry death of God
How loud I cry that hulk is truly shattered
Showing the vascular burning ship and vessel
In which the screaming Nietsche has been martyred.
O lacerations multiply! O thousand tongues
Affirm in the despairing hymns of blood
That, like a right rolling among its wrongs,
My God is dead, but his death can wrestle.

What liberty we know among the stars
No, is not liberty but a pillar to post
Mopping and mowing of a cause that lost
Its way and will boxing the compassed stars
That now at half mast mourn over the vast
Dead sea of the dead god of the dead stars.

III.

Answer me, answer me, Siren of negation!
Whose face of mystery gazes from the mirror
When we are out of the room? What voice
Invokes a divine verb which we cannot hear?
O globe that shatters at the exultation
Of what we know we know. O perfect error
Proud in your pound of flesh, rejoice, rejoice:
Until that birth the unknown god slept here.

From the red worm inside a blind eye
She shall emerge in all her invisible splendour,
The vestal of negation, the sibyl of absence,
And uttering the first anepiac cry
Shatter the categories of asserted grandeur
And to what is not delegate transcendence.

Verses for the 60th Birthday of Thomas Stearns Eliot

1.
By that evening window where
His accurate eye keeps Woburn Square
Under perpetual judgement so
That only the happy can come and go
About these gardens and not be
Tested in that dark neutrality,
Which, in between love and disgust,
Hates most of all its own mistrust,
I see this gentle and gothic man
Tame Apollyon with a pen.

2.
I never know the juggernauts
Go bulldozing through my thoughts
So that everything I own
Is trod down and overthrown
So that everything I own
Is trod down and overthrown
Without remembering that worse
Than thunder in the hearse
Is the supernatural sigh
Of illusions as they die—
But in the room of Eliot
The visions whistle as they rot.

3.
To him the dead twig in the gutter
Cries across all law to utter
Confidences that would bring
Tears to the eyes of anything.
But that set imperial face
Has looked down on our disgrace
And, without betraying so
Little as a twinge of sorrow,

Seen all grief begin again—
A gentle and long-suffering man.

4.
Outside the huge negations pass
Like whirlwinds writing on the grass
Inscriptions teaching us that all
The lessons are ephemeral;
But as the huge negations ride
And depredate all things outside
His window, he puts out his hand
And writes with whirlwinds on the ground
Asseverations that tame
The great negations with his name.

Epitaph for the Poet

The single sleeper lying here
   Is neither lying nor asleep.
Bend down your nosey parker car
   And eavesdrop on him. In the deep
Conundrum of the dirt he speaks
   The one word you will never hear.

Memorial Inscription

O Leopardi! O Lion-pawed Seas!
Give tongue, give tongue, against, again
The mistress of all miseries
The master of all mysteries.
O Lion-pawed heart! O voices of stone!
Shatter the tabernacle in which we grieve,
Crack the mad jacket in which we rejoice
   Alive for ever alone!

Galway Bay

With the gulls' hysteria above me
I walked near these breakneck seas
This morning of mists, and saw them,
Tall the mysterious queens
Waltzing in on the broad
Ballroom of the Atlantic.

All veils and waterfalls and
Wailings of the distraught,
These effigies of grief moved
Like refugees over the water;
The icy empresses of the Atlantic
Rising to bring me omen.

These women woven of ocean
And sorrows, these far sea figures,
With the fish and skull in their
Vapour of faces, the icicles
Salting down from their eyelashes,
As I walked by the foreshore

Moved towards me, ululating:
O dragnet of the sweet heart
Bind us no longer! The cage
Bursts with passions and bones,
And every highspirited fish
Lives off our scuttled love!

I stood on a stone, the gulls
Crossed my vision with wings
And my hearing with caterwauling;
The hurdling wave, backbroken,
Died at my feet. Taller
Than the towering hour above me

The homing empresses of the sea
Came among me. And, shivering,

I felt death nuzzling in the nest
Of the diurnally shipwrecked
Drowned nocturnally breast.

Zennor Idyl I

Let me establish in the bitter line
The empire of that affection every creature
Keeps as its only kingdom in the winter
Of the world as it is. Lonely by water
I bear your faces corniced at my shoulder
When I look down, dogged and ragged by disgraces
I cannot contend with alone. This afternoon
You, my sweet friends, are gone, and I sit now
Watching the vacant day pursue its ends
To bright rage twisting in the quiet sky.
Now you are gone. Can these words assuage
That gross worm in the heart whom only death
Ever stood nearer to? The monster in a storm
Is always us. Apollyon down a well
Chimes and is tame at a hand. O gentle
Five thousand fish spawned by the name
Any cold heart is cut to, never diminish
Your miraculous multiplication of stars
The loving shall people. What debars the supreme
Virtue who shakes her symbols in my dreams
Save, behemoth walking and talking in all storms,
I, whom the thundering heart, the talk of lightning
Forms and deforms. I turn my head
And where your voices yoked that friendly urn
I keep a death in, now, bleeding to bull,
The truly beautiful is my prey and feeding.
Seven worded in the breast my love is broken
Where a hand rested. But the token stone
Prize of all the ego's coldest prizes,
Rises and rises through seas and eyes

Till its red penny entablatures every child
And the androgynous worm is exiled. So you, this afternoon,
Picking like birds over the walls and moors
Leave me to the sad talking of my thoughts
Over the ulcerous poem. But I have had
That consolation the world has also known—
A triumph of crowns stuck in the memory—crowns,
O spikes, O fading faces, and, over the hill,
The lover of all shall meet the lover of all.

Zennor Idyl II

Towards what landlocked summer sidling like swans
Will our love move us in those feathered bridals
The innocent, the beautiful and the good so briefly
Know before their unfolding leaf is fallen
The ring of roses is wrung. Rainspoiled an hour
Erases the bunch of pouting and kissing images;
Shouting the crossed lives wrestle in the sky
And westward a memory carries all love away.

Never return again, never return again,
Desire for what is gone. And in the wild
Winds of the memory, then, great thistles toss
Their hair and lash the recollection
Till the granite that groans inside us weeps. Where
Lost now on rainswept yesterday loiter
The once bright bathers in my blue eye?
O mackintoshed figures shouldering through clouds

Along a skyline of remembrance, forget
The hour I housed you in my sheet and shackle
Forget, forget the knot and the cup of kindness—
For the knot will stick like a rock in the loving
Cup of the heart, and break it. Let the clock
Wipe clear the face turned back toward such times

And circumvent regret. Climb the morning hill
Into cold rain, drop the iron chain of flowers,
Leave in the valley those hours that live a fable
Voicing for ever a vocable that cannot die.

Songs for Sailors

I.

As I was walking along by the Embankment
I heard a drowned man calling out of the dark,
"Stay away, stay away, all the women are fishes,
And my son's being strung up in Battersea Park."

"The suckers in blue sail away on their coffins,
And the rocks that I played on when I was a kid,
Gone under the death that is rolling me over.
Everything grieves me that I ever did.

"From islands where niggers squat on their fat bottoms,
From the pearl-handled shores and the dove-voiced trees,
I can hear the sweet songs of the boys, but their eyes are
As cold and as bitter as these salt seas."

II.

Call, call so softly to me over the loud
    Oceans between us
That I may hear your spindrift voice beneath
    The seas' hyenas.

And tell me, tell me again you chiding keep
    Deep in your breast
My xiphiac transfixions where you sleep
    But never rest.

That Laddie's a Long Way from Home

That laddie's a long way from home, who loved
    Nothing the least
And everything most of all. He found
    The whole world best.

He went away to put his sweet arm around
    The star's waist,
And to give the glad eye to the Seven Sisters
    Who wink in the West.

When he whistled at the wide world she took him
    Close to her breast,
O that laddie's a long way from home, and long
    Long will he rest.

In Memory of a Friend

The fury this Friday broke through my wall
  With a death certificate in its hand.
Bright, bright, Elipsion, burn tonight
  Across the sky and tell the whole
Empty and insignificant world that I grieve
  For a tall Jack with the sun on his wrist
And a sky stuffed up his sleeve. Let me leave
  Love on the mantelpiece looking East
To gather together the dust that I have lost.

They walk in silence over the same spaces
  Where they once talked, and now do not,
The dumb friends with the whitewashed faces
  Who lifted a hand and died. They forget us
In the merciful amnesia of their death,
  But by us, the disremembered, they cannot
Ever be forgotten. For, always, in all places,
  They will rise eloquently up to remind us
Of the unforgettable allegiances behind us.

My love, my love, why do you leave me alone?
   My love, my love, where, where are you gone?
Here the tall altitudes grieve as they gaze down
   Knowing that you, elusive their lover, are gone,
And that you will never again
   Kiss the teeth of the morning at a vivid four hundred,
Uncurling, at nine angels, the gold and splendid
   Wake on which you walk across the sky.
Grieving, like them, I cannot believe it is ended.

Remember the eye that haunts me for ever
   Wherever I am under any sky,
O completely from leaf and smiling from over
   Every horizon he looks at me.
The simple sea shall fold its wide arms
   Less long about the world
Than I shall hold him in my dreams
   Until every moment seems
To reclaim part of him.

The salt that at the lashes of
   All Seven Seas laces the shores
Grazing my weeping eye of sores,
   Engenders the more of love.
Here by the salt tide at the South
   That washes its coils along
The coast that lies behind the eyes,
   His wreck is like a rock in my mouth
With his body on my tongue.

Time with its shoving shall unsmooth
   The brightest lying lover
And in the teeth of human truth
   Prove that the heart needs more than faith
To help it to recover
   The love that took a look at death
And promised me forever:
   As, under Northern Seas, his face
Fades as the seas wash over.

My love, my love, lift up your joystick hand.
   Dismiss the dividing
Grief. Bring, bring again the kiss and the guiding
   Glory. From his hiding
Place in the cleft of the cloud, O dove of evening,
   Lead him back over that dark intervening
Day when he died. Lead him back in a loving
   Return to that room where I
Look out and see his death glittering in the sky.

The killers shall spring into each other's arms
   And the storms subside:
The catalytical shall kiss, and the relief
   Wrap cities in mutual belief
And the dove preside.
   Then all but this tall one and the dead
Shall feel the warming of the world
   Running through every board and bed
Colder because they died.

Sleep, long and beautiful, in that bag
   Where loneliness, my tall falcon,
Shall never again cheat you with the mirage
   Of sensual satisfaction.
Look, look, the grave shakes over his head
   And the red dirt stands up, as
Across existence I beg him heed:
   To those that love there are no dead,
Only the long sleepers.

Elegy on the Death of Michael Roberts

How dare the greatest die? For whom else daily
   Will water and wilderness come down to us with bread?
Where is the hole in the world proud enough to keep
   Him deep in the grave of the gravelled dead:
While about his skull, coiling, the unsaid poems vainly

   Mourn, and in his schoolroom the fooling
Truth ogles a mirror and forgets that eagled head?

So wasteful the world is with her few of best.
   O pinnacles where the elected princes die
With their dogstar boots on and a truth in hand,
   O tabernacles glittering to attest
So few have ever ascended so far or so high,
   O Michael's bone enshrined in altitude,
Truth is meridian to tempt kings to try.

The proud ride past us on their hippogryphs
   To lazy empires opulent with trophies
Others caught up from the holocaust and the hazards
   At what a price. I saw you stride across
A Fitzroy room and leave, stamped on the boards,
   In the nailed image heroes and poems possess,
A symbol of spirit that did not call for words,

And skulled as aquiline as the two-headed Maximus
   You, Michael, also. Gazing towards the left
You leaned a shoulder against the ideal azimuth
   And theories shook their seven veils and laughed.
You turned your head to the principle of right
   And a principle came down to earth and performed:
So you were active a man and a teacher, formed
   Together, and the poem walked upright.

But can the harp shoot through its propellers? At heart
   There was an Orphic unicorn in his chest
Who, dying, drove the spindle through his breast
   And both of them died. O he unsung apart
The Siamese master who could daydream and act:
   He would not let his harpstrung fellow sing
And so the poet choked him with a fact.

He lolled against a mantelpiece, and a tree
   Of lovingkindness sprouted in the grate,
Catching all friends up in its talkative branches
   As the bright bird's-eye glittered behind glass.

Too seldom, I know now, I watched this face
   Talk through the truth like a ship through the sea,
With the noumena tying roses on the anchors
   And the anchors conquering the great sea.

How dare the greatest die? They do not die.
   Over my writing shoulder, now, guiding
As many before he guided, head and master, with all
   The teaching fathers fit for such presiding,
He returns when the poem comes down from the sky
   With the truth in its claws. The best of all
Teach us that death is no easy place of hiding.
   But an everest where, higher, the greater fall.

On the approaching Birth of a Child to Friends

(*For Donald and Rene Horwood*)

How, among this universe
Of the worst generating worse
Can I cry a welcoming?

Happy now he lies in water
Who shall lie in your arms later
And weep at that awakening.

Who was I, the genes murmur
Sprang like a salmon up my mother
To clasp a cross of grieving.

Ask the undammed and damned womb:
Why was it a black lamb whom
You marked for mothering?

Orpheus, all are orphan. Alone
We seek reversion to the one
Who died at our beginning.

Dear lovers, carrying, like a vase
Birth among the anarchic stars
And they go down blundering

Through pandemonium, to dead end,
You move and love and so forfend
Some human suffering.

The child is born of its own will.
We are automata. But it's an ill
Wind without some smiling.

Your son, in his own good time,
Will generate the natural crime
And learn about forgiving.

Your daughter, with the cause the same,
Seeing all things multiply, blame
Nothing for multiplying.

It is our cause. What can we say
Once we have loved? We must obey
Living, and loving, and dying.

The Weepers in the Sacred Tree

Weeping, they spoke out of the sacred tree:
  'Dark and unloving powers
Envying everything valuable that is ours
  Determine human destiny.'

Smiling, they stroked the bird on my shoulder.
  'Bright bait,' they cried, 'Virtue!
Bringing down hammer and lightning upon the
    upholder.
The dove shall desert you.'

Sighing, they showed anguish in their breast:
  'Look! Look!' they cried.
'The pain is eternal but the cause has died.
  Who cares what is best!'

Waiting for peace a victim at my foot
  Turned to stone with patience.
The voices murmured: 'Bitter the bitter fruit
  Of our supplications.'

Then out of the tongue-twisting tree spoke to me
  Every human and animal:
'We ask our parental cause why we had to be.
  Why do we live at all?'

'Why do the bright-eyed algae fold the shore
  Unloving in their embrace?
O unrewarded servants of Time and Place,
  Serve, serve no more.'

'Shuddering the great star uncurls at its sex
  In labour, but cannot give
Back in the teeth of the universal multiplex
  A stellar negative.'

'O brute and hour, tooth and knife,
  Condemned to live and suffer and never die,
Pronounce the unholy Why.
  Root out the assent at the source of life.'

Subsiding the weeping ceased in the sacred tree
  As the leaves closed over
And I saw the everlastingly restless body of humanity
  Clasped in the sins of its lover.

Goodman Jacksin and the Angel

ANGEL.

Thus, Goodman Jacksin, time has come
For truth in cockleshells and nuts;
I beg you leave your head and home,
Come, cut the cackle, (cackle cuts)
And to the catchpenny cosmos show
The vipers nuzzling in your guts
And my tall spectres shaped of snow.

JACKSIN.

What, get down off the five-barred star
To let a bullying gale blow in?
I know what kind of a rogue you are,
When I step out, you will step in.
There are no matters, to my mind,
Worth any labour in the mouthing:
I'll just sit here on my behind—
All your wind amounts to nothing.

ANGEL.

Look, Farmer Cynic, chips are down.
The scarecrows howl about the hills,
Clocks gaze in crystals, fishes drown,
It's more than a cold wind that kills.
O bullyboy, leave the two-headed self
To peep both ways with a knowing leer;
The world is still your better half,
And it's not somewhere else—it's here.

JACKSIN.

I'm not the man for you, my stranger.
I've got my hands quite full enough.
I bow my head at my soul's anger
And when I've got a cold I cough.
Leave well, that's me, leave well alone.
Why come to pester us with these

Cold questions set too near the bone?
What's it to me if angels freeze?

ANGEL.
What's it if this sanctuary,
The holy of the holy heart
Where, paraclete in an aviary,
The mind beatifies every part
That goes to make a singing soul—
What's it to you if this bright temple
Is split in two from pole to pole?
Well, what's an earthquake, for example?

JACKSIN.
With these bright eyes I have witnessed
What the bright ploughshare also sees;
The running generations harnessed
In green laws to divine decrees:
The seeding generations under
Every winter solstice stir,
And, from the earth at a dead end,
A daughter rise up, praising her.

ANGEL.
My Goodman Jacksin, for this prize,
This curious privilege of dirt,
You, man of clay, yes, bright of eyes,
Are but responsible in part.
A very little part. You lay
Your rag and bone down in a grave
To fructify dirt in a way—
But this is all the part you have.

JACKSIN.
Angelic Cynic, sing to me
Of all my greater purposes—
Apocalypse I die to see,
That allegory that always is

Rising up through obscurities
To dazzle my bright eyes:
O revelation of verities
Whose loving never dies.

ANGEL.

What abstract crackpot could so love
You, goodman jacksin, straw in hair,
You, with all pigeons and no dove,
You Monday hound and Sunday hare,
You, axing oracles with a fact—
With you, part mud and three parts water,
What heavenly vision, now or later,
The rainbow covenant will contract?

JACKSIN.

I tell you, Angel, that gods die,
Princes and gross empires pass,
But the bright stars of heaven shall
Rotate for ever in my arse.
The hand that turns the zodiac
In its great circle over all,
Is the horned fist of a husband jack
With a bright eye on the ball.

ANGEL.

Honouring itself the clay rears up
To praise its pottering purposes,
But, oh, much sorrow shall it sup
Before fulfilment is.
That Dagon slumbers in every seed
Who shall rise up and rend,
Then you shall need a friend indeed
But find a fiend instead.

JACKSIN.

I wake on mornings in the winter
With the holy snow on the ground,
I see the hoofmarks milling round
Where nightlong in the cattle pound

I and the cloven fiend, hellbound,
Wrestle together, without a sound,
For the white world that sleeps around
As we rage in the centre.

ANGEL.

The rooftops bear his sinning track!
His goat-hooves outrage bed and birth!
O draw the sheet over the earth—
I see the horn begin to jack
Against all daughters of innocence!
O Goodman Jacksin, underneath
The sweet dream and the simple sense,
His hunting semen ferrets death.

JACKSIN.

You rave like any soapbox gabber.
Evil is simply this, my friend:
A good we do not understand.
Right at the heart of all this blabber
The good is matching with the bad,
But which is which, O angel-demon,
What final proof was ever had?
What's the issue of your semen?

ANGEL.

At the living centre of all this,
Evil and good, in expiation,
Dovetail the great antithesis
As they clasp round the ends of creation:
As when, in winter, through a window,
A sad man sees the sun endow
The skeleton of his private sorrow
A bedizening transfiguration.

JACKSIN.

You, Jew jumped up from an ilex tree,
Who gave you this heartburn of laurels?
An old man whom I cannot see,
A fathering farmer of farrows,

With his blackjack spade, a gun on his knee,
And his everlasting quarrels:—
I like my money no more than he
Loves his pocketful of morals.

ANGEL.

You see your youngest son at dawn
Stalk out into eerie mist,
A strapping strider, a man born
An Adam from the first:—
But darkly in the devoted mind
You dog him from his chancy cradle
In dread that, laid out on a hurdle,
He will come back—to the ground.
Jehovah also saw you stride
Out of a green and guarded gate
Into the mystery of your fate:
He too felt the crossbone shadow ride
The stalking horse of his heart,
As, tracking, anxious, secret, saw
The hounds of hell rout out and start
All the sorrow you were born for.

JACKSIN.

Red, red the daybreak when I rose
To find I was the son
Of that far loving father whose
Son is as sad as my own.
I would not have the half of my grief
Put upon beast or god,
No, leave to me the best belief:
My sorrow is the greatest.

ANGEL.

Goodman Jacksin, Jacksin Goodman,
You burn the twisted auburn leaves,
Thinking, like any other woodman,
"The leaves are like ourselves."
The splintered glitter of the dead,
And the falling heroes of melancholy,

Do they not serve, in her holy bed,
The mother of all that is holy?

JACKSIN.
O crystal and snow-hearted eagle
Inhabit the hills of my soul
So that I too, like a sexless angel,
May see things from a better angle
And lose the heart in the whole,
Not in the cellar of a single
Consecration but nailed out
On the vast edges of all doubt.

ANGEL.
The androgynous worm and I
Your guardian arable and green,
Like caryatids hold up between
Us all oppositions under the sky.
Seraphic I take to my breast
The basilisk spirallings of the lie,
Only to find I rock to rest
The dove in a dichotomy.

JACKSIN.
The adultress shall have such sweet dreams
That the babe in her arms will smile:
As, by apparent accident,
Evolving through the obscure schemes
Of our spiritual systems,
Obvious Evil, as it seems,
Emerges, in a little while,
Redeemed, and white, and provident.

ANGEL.
The laws of act and consequence
Obey a justice none
May follow with a rational sense—
For it is not our own.
Odylic engines of destiny
Who can say what will come

From the venially inserted penny—
What Juggernauts roll in time?

JACKSIN.
I watch boys chasing butterflies
Among the summer hedges:
I hear their high and hunting cries
As the sky-blown flier dodges
Between their hands, till, in disguise
Against the dog-rose lodges.
Then they stand silent by the rose
To see a rainbow close its wings.

ANGEL.
And out of the horn rumpled sheet
Where nightlong in their forking lock
The hissing kissers slew and mock
That image from which they were cast—
Out of that fouled and rocking nest
In which those justly outcast meet
And mount like stray dogs in the street,—
Out, out the innocent image steps.

JACKSIN.
O Minotaur! A maze! A maze!
We only know what we have done
And through what hecatombs have been
When, there before us, we come upon
Bleeding our crying footprints run
Across, ahead. And we have seen
The lost tracks, like a fugitive son,
Of some long forgotten cause.

ANGEL.
The falling feather can engender
By no known laws of heredity
A generation of clashing rocks:
And conceptions of great spiritual splendour
Derive, through successions of paradox,
From brief moments of cheap misery;

Just as the flat and selfish sea
Has set a crowned amoeba free.

JACKSIN.
Or sewing the sweet thistledown sigh
Reap whirlwinds in a daughter womb,
And never know whose exiled cry
Unlooses on us, worlds away,
This avalanche of vinculum
As, idle in a drawing room,
We watch the goldfinch prisoner die
As this silent ghost goes by.

ANGEL.
So, ruddy husbandman, foot of clay,
I too am a dog's demigod,
And tell you, majesty of mud,
That neither you nor I can say
Where the first fault really lay.
But all those living creatures who
Inherit, just because they live,
The property of error—O forgive!

JACKSIN.
Come, petty parson, that's much better.
But let me butt in with a word:
I'm not the postman with a black letter,
I'm not the vengeance of the Lord
Engaged in some small-time vendetta—
Come, tell me, which of us, in truth,
Could ever really forgive the other?
And who could ever forgive us both?

ANGEL.
My guilt shines in the glittering
Perennial and praying tree,
That, without dropping on its knee,
Praises never flattering.
The shame of angels is their love
Must so abase itself before

That hallelujah they adore,—
Has more idolatry than love.

JACKSIN.
And yet what can we do if we are
Swept up in such a storm of wings
As that authoritative power—
What do save cower in our fear?
Then in that bosomed and huge cave
Crouch, trusting that our cooing love
Declare in fear and tremblings:
We are crushed out by that thunder?

ANGEL.
O let the shivering leaf disclose
The susurrus of that solicitude
Not stirs the feather on a wren
But cools the rotors of the stars.
That giant sleeps in molecules
And exercises in iotas
The earthquake of his regimen
On pismires of all magnitude.

JACKSIN.
I saw the spawning fishes write
My guilt shine on the water's bed;
Yes, too much love, like you, my friend,
I also gave; but O to what?
Not the landlord of the infinite,
(So deeply in his debt I stand)
But to all living things instead
We give the love that is not ours.

ANGEL.
She shakes the winged horse in his stall
For her you break your roots and walk
Water to clasp snakes and trees;
All living things obey her: all
Support each other for their own sake.
Then as, on those maternal knees,

Sit sucking at that happy milk,
Forget a father got all these.

JACKSIN.
Thus the antinomy of love
Inverts its propositions. We
—Fourteen stone and an Idea—
Turned tables turtle truly have.
The sibyl trudges through my mud
To show me her humility,
And I trapeze on a dizzy cloud
To teach Azrafel not to fear.

ANGEL.
In the arched dialectic by
Which all existence must evolve,
There is no wallflower at the dance,
On all things that first law devolves.
And thus the innocent must die
Because its very innocence
By law of opposition calls
The skulls to lead it in that dance.

JACKSIN.
There is no mystery in this
A man and woman do not know:
The law of dialectics is
How Love evolves. There are no
Two ones of any kind but must
Bring forth a firstborn third to prove
That the arithmetic of love
Transcends our lonely dust.

ANGEL.
Thus Love and Death together got
Under a dark constellation,
And in their fever they forgot
That even Love and Death are not
Exempt from generation.
Then from their open-eyed embrace

Rose the first god that ever was,
With doom in his face.

JACKSIN.
How shall I speak of mystery
With a gun and a pound in my hand?
I must obey a master I
Shall never understand.
All flesh is grass, all grass is flesh
And the midnight sun roars down:
I and my soul go up in a flash,
I and my soul go down.

Consolatory Verses for the Middle Years

Rose I this morning for the first day of Spring
  And saw was gone
The poor white litter of the bareboned king
  Not from the mind alone
But lifted that cold law from every thing—
  From every deadlocked form
  Of beast, idea and stone:
And I no longer boy still seek to affirm.

And I no longer boy still seek to find
  That sacred instrument—
The haunted chord struck by a dawn wind
  Which by presentiment
Of breath lifts the dead feathers of the mind
  Exalting a transcendent.
So, holy poem, I seek the idea enshrined
  With all altared thought,
And bleeding eagles, as they strike to blind,
  Shall tear a vision out.

To dedicate, O Pythia, to your greater power
  The no longer easy

Paean and praise of a heavier heart and hour
    I with this poem essay.
Still will the clouded hand or downcast bird
    Rise up from under
The gravelled spirit, and, not by a grave deterred,
    Honour the Pythian splendour.

When princes asphyxiate themselves for private reasons
    What can the rest of us do?
There is no rest. Such princes in their passions
    Are dead pilots who
Teach us what not to do. From their gaudy lessons
    Retrieve the knowledge
That tall men walk upright in lightning because
    It calls for more courage.

To a Child

By the mad dead Moon
And carrioned ghats of day
With frenzied the skeleton
That shakes like Death at play
Under ground everyone
And across the hissing sea
That coils like eyes between
All that we have been
And all that we wish to be,
I crossed everything and nothing
At the red pit of Time
With a wolf in a word's clothing
And the snake-locked image of dream
Hanging ahead, until
The stone-hinged circle came
Round as I stood still
And face to face a child
And I stood double there,
A wild and silent pair
A pair crying and mild.

Letter to a Young Poet

There is that whispering gallery where
A dark population of the air
Gives back to us those vocables
We dare not robe in syllables:

I speak of the whispering gallery
Of all Dionysian poetry
Within whose precincts I have heard
An apotheosis of the word

As down those echoing corridors
The Logos rode on a white horse;
Till every No that sense could express
Turned to a transcendental Yes.

Sanctified by such passages
Let us exchange our messages,
And, as we walk, all enigmas
Describe themselves in terms of stars.

From those lyrical waterfalls rise
Words that bring rainbows to the eyes
And memories called up from the ground
Smile to see their blood around.

There is a spirit of turbulence
Inhabiting the intelligence
Determined always to impose
Another reason on the rose

Another cause upon the creature
Than the privilege of its nature;
A handcuff and a history
Upon all natural mystery

And this turbulent spirit starts
That insurrection in our hearts

By which the laws of poetry
Are broken into anarchy:

The anarchy that seeks to show
An altitude which way to go,
Or use astronomy to prove
That duty is our only love.

But over the known world of things
The great poem folds its wings
And from a bloody breast will give
Even to those who disbelieve.

By the known world the intellect
Stands with its bright gun erect,
But the long loving verities
Are kissing at the lattices.

That dark population of the air
Leans downward, singing, to declare
The mystery of the world is this:
That we do not know what is.

At the Wake of Dylan Thomas

I cannot take, even for such a purpose
As to honour this death by act of passion,
The word that wore the ring of his married breath.

I will not, where she clasps that curly nothing
Darkly in tears apart and the Dragon mourning,
Vex his cold nurse with a fragmentation of heart.

The vocable flies crying back into September
Away from my hand rather than remember
That speech, like a nagging wife, has been abandoned

By that master of the house so early waking
That the worm and the first bird found him larking
In a Welsh dawn with the paraclete of the word.

The air is full of dead verbs. There are ashes
In every dumbstruck mouth as the dead tide washes
Salt into the ulcer of a torn-out truth.

The merman floats face down on the sea of a poem.
The fish that flew from Wales to the back of doom
Lies cold on the stone of silence. The sea prevails.

Silence is what we hear in the roaring shell.
That first sea whence we rose and to which shall
Go down when all the words and all the heroes

Striking their lyres and attitudes in the middle
Of that burning sea which was a cradle,
Go down under that silence of that sea.

This son of pearl was walking beside water
Taking the pain of sand out of the oyster:
"We will make poems," he said, "simply from joy."

And with the same wonder that the first amoeba
Stepped out of hydrogen and saw God's labour,
He goggled at glory as though it had just begun.

That burning babe! Crying from a bushel
Where he hid all his knowledge in the vessel
Of a divine and a divining image,

He triumphed up the trumpets of a cherub.
What is more for ever and more terrible
Than Abraham's kid and babe singing together?

Where there is a world of wise-eyed infants
Whose innocence has survived all living onslaughts
So that they always look newly arrived:

That cloudy boy harping among the graves
Will lead a doxological choir of loves.
O the dirt sings because all joy is magical.

What is the age of the one who never grieves
But to whom even Grief looks up and gives
An eye as green and new as an Eden leaf?

He is as old as that forsaken garden
Where only he and all the spellbound children
May freely in delight forget a fall.

That corpse of curls! O Dionysian
You will not come back through the door marked Man.
You went the wrong way. And the dawn was black.

But will the bird of fire submit to a lock and key?
The curls dance round the black cap and are free.
And any warty boy can double back.

Blind Harry and Sandy Traill before us
Showed that simply by dying we add to the manic chorus
And put the fear of God up all surviving.

And now he's gotten, first of all and foremost,
You, Dylan, too, the one undoubting Thomas,
The whistler in the dark he's taken from us.

Is it you, Cymric, or I who am so cold?
Was it a word and world America killed?
The brainstruck harp lies with its bright wings furled.

And as the winter closes coldly around
This puzzled and bitter necrosis of ground,
The images of death begin to glitter

Like falling icicles of an immanent
End. But I have known, for a moment,
The I undead and the dead who was my friend

Change places. Thus, if this poem speaks
A crown of joy or courage among cold rocks,
It is his spirit that animates my language.

Not in peace rest this whistling jaw now shall
But call and cry from every highblown hill:
"My voice and my grave open. I cannot die."

But his ghost puts by this poem and goes down
Shaking its locks loudly into the dark,
And every word of the tongue follows him proudly.

Channel Crossing

To John Lehmann

And just by crossing the short sea
To find the answer sitting there
Combing out its snaky hair
And with a smile regarding me
Because it knows only too well
That I shall never recognize
The axioms that I should prize
Or the lies that I should tell.

I saw the question in the sky
Ride like a gull to fool me, as
The squat boat butted at the seas
As grossly as through ultimates I
Churn up a frothy wake of verbs
Or stir a muddy residue
Looking for that answer who
Sanctifies where she perturbs.

The horror of the questionmark
I looked back and saw stand over

The white and open page of Dover
Huge as the horn of the scapegoat. Dark
It stood up in the English day
Interrogating Destiny
With the old lip of the sea:
"What can a dead nation say?"

As these words wailed in the air
I looked at Europe and I saw
The glittering instruments of war
Grow paler but not go from where
Like a Caesarian sunset on
The cold slab of the horizon
They lay foretelling for tomorrow
Another day of human sorrow.

But when I turned and looked into
The silent chambers of the sea
I saw the displaced fishes flee
From nowhere into nowhere through
Their continent of liberty.
O skipping porpoise of the tide
No longer shall the sailors ride
You cheering out to sea.

I thought of Britain in its cloud
Chained to the economic rocks
Dying behind me. I saw the flocks
Of great and grieving omens crowd
About the lion on the stone.
And I heard Milton's eagle mewing
Her desolation in the ruin
Of a great nation, alone.

That granite and gigantic sigh
Of the proud man beaten by
Those victories from which we die;
The gentle and defeated grief
Of the gale that groans among
Trees that are a day too strong

And, victorious by a leaf,
Show the winner he was wrong.

The continent of discontent
Rose up before me as I stood
Above the happy fish. Endued
With hotter and unhappier blood
Contented in my discontent,
I saw that every man's a soul
Caught in the glass wishing bowl:
To live at peace in discontent.

O somewhere in the seven leagues
That separate us from the stricken
Amphitheatre of the spirit,
O somewhere in that baleful sea
The answer of sad Europe lodges,
The clue that causes us to sicken
Because we cannot find and share it,
Or, finding, cannot see.

So in the sky the monstrous sun
Mocked like a punishment to be,
Extending, now, to you and me
The vision of what we have done:
And as the boat drew to the quay
I thought, by crossing the short water
I shall not find, in its place,
The answer with a silent face.

At the Tombs of the Medici

(*For the Quincentenary of Lorenzo dei Medici*)

Open this empty house to those
Who knock upon the dreaming skull
Not with a hand or tear but with
The crossed keys of a proper love:
Open the empty grave and show
What mansions and what miracles
Glitter within the bone that sleeps,
What glories agonize in this stone.

Too long in sepulchres you rest;
Rise, rise and rage you effigies
Who taught the anthropoid to sing
And ruled the liar with a smile:
Too long have rested in these tombs
The splendid eagle in his chains,
The bald, black-handed extrovert
And the gun loaded with a rose.

O never intellect like a boat
Swanned sweeter through a bitter sea
Than when this ugly duckling with
A broken nose walked water here:
And seated in a garden chair
Looked up at politics and smiled:
"Because all things obey the soul
There is no rain. But love is here."

The lily in the valley lifts
Its golden crest above the streets
Where, dead as any derelict,
The flowered city droops in sleep:
So down among the dead men he
Dreams under Buonarotti's stone,
A pinch of dirt but taller than
The fallen ball or the Apennine.

What, huddled up in bloody marble,
So shakes this spirit in its grave
That as I stand against this kingdom
I feel the rock shake with his rage?
That raging of the greater man
Who, looking down on what he made,
Sees the bright crown a cuspidor,
And the idea begging at the gate.

Peace is always a lie. Always
The catchpenny cut-throat is elect.
Most of the world is dirt. No less
Cheat and liar rule from the grave.
So aggravate his unsleeping heart
The white-tongued worm and coiling fake:
This sweating and unsceptred king
What rest could take in any tomb?

The anarchist stalks across the sky,
The double cross divides and shines;
The rat and ass cohabit: the whores
Of economics kiss and kill.
The greatest and the best, those powers
Of Justice and of Truth, now lie
Under this stone, under this empty stone
By which I sorrow over a living man.

The Dying and Heroic Captives of Italy

To Robert Colquhoun

What we thought and what we said
Can really be known only by
Those rooted caryatids that stand
Upholding the individual mind;
And, sometimes, grinding in despair
At being so predial there,

Open granite lips to call
To every soul of living rock
Walled up in a wailing gaol.

I thought as I stood by this tomb
That the cold dead quiet there
Were no more isolated from
Each other than the living here:
I lift a hand of paper to
You in your exercise of dust
And if a little love gets through
Then we are luckier than most.
Our incommunicable unicorn
Never to be seen or known
Lifts its glass horn to everyone,
Until, so fabulously alone,
We wish we never had been born.
And so I write these lines, Colquhoun,
To wave a heart to you across
That desert vaster than the moon
Separating each one of us:
That waste where a dawn mirage
Deludes us for a moment we
May lift our dirty eyes and see
Love and its knee-rocking image.

Then as the posing statues, covered
With admiration like thin slime
Trudged off, but left to be discovered
Their plaster stand-ins serving time,
So we, honouring the still dead,
Unharried left them sleeping in
That peace so strenuously won.
Let Alighieri close his stark
Volcanic eye unvexed by those
Myopic vultures of the dark
Who watch that huge corpse decompose.

O aerial Fiesole
Love lives in your olive tree,

For underneath it I have heard
The carillon and blinded bird
Of that gold, forgotten word
In exaltation. The stolid Fates
To whom the unknown arbitrates
Know, now, that we have cheated them
With a glimpse of the sworded garden
That will sustain us, and redeem
The miseries we cannot pardon.

Stanzas on a Visit to Longleat House in Wiltshire, October 1953

To John Farrelly

Dead pomp sneering underground
Glares up at a horned foot of clay
Where the hog of multitude hangs around
Among these tremendous memories
That delegate to our day
The superannuated and damned glories.

A quidnunc with a shopping bag
Stops gossiping with another hag
And where immense conceptions were
Dragged shrieking from their cellars here
The ragged-arsed mechanics squat
Owning what they haven't got.

O rare rain of disinterest
Descend on this fouled public nest
And rout out all vulgarities
That, crowding through its majesties,
Gut to bare shell and bone
The grandeur of the dead and gone.

In car-park, garden and urinal
The free and ignorant, almost
As easy as at a Cup Final
Gawk through the stone-transparent ghost
Of this once noble house, now lost
In the gross error of survival.

"Come," said my proud and sulking friend,
"Four angels up to Heaven's Gate,
And looking down at Longleat
So far below, shall disappear
The human termite, leaving there
Stones and spectres hand in hand."

And from that aerial sweep of height
The valley fell through depths if pine
Down through green distances until
From glimmering water rising bright
Longleat, bird's-eyed in sunshine,
Smiled up from its own funeral.

I saw the heroic seizins fade
And hide in laurels of old trees
As brassbands of indignities
Exploded echoes to degrade
The splendours and the miseries
Of that cold illustrious shade.

The Mnemonic Demigod

To fly from the crying ghost
Here I have come to hide
A hope and a heart that shake
In those tempests of memories
That living and loving evoke.
Wild, wild wind of what was
Dart through a breast and bone

Crying remember! Crying
Never remember never,
For the dead sing on the rocks
Of glittering recollection
And every human seaman
Smiling would die to recapture
Those so utterly beloved
And utterly lost. Great seas
Moan in a child's shell
And all time in a single
Memory. Here by a wood
With Aldworth over my head
I have laid down my board
And made a bed. The wind
Hums sullenly among
The ash and the sadder alder
Till I can hear again
Those heart-breaking voices
Rise like swans out of every
Harp of the summer wood
And every organ and leaf
Of body and mind. Cease,
Victims, victors of love,
And leave in the evening
The unlonely I alone.
O wilder worlds and wilder
Space fly crying from
That star behind the face
Where all wrongs begin.
There is that universe
Turning behind the eyes
That rolls its proud wheels
Through our remorse and over
The thousand shouting corpses
Whom no remorse revives.
Sweep, sweep across the sky
Red blizzard of the heart
Exact one withering stroke
From the thunderhead of
Remembered love. The dogs

Whine at a broken gate
As the three-headed huntsman
Hounds us down. My love,
My love has hidden tomorrow
In a wood that I cannot see,
And all that I can find
Is echoes, echoes. This stream
By which my old house stands
Like a water of faces
Speaks and accuses me
With a perpetual wringing of wrongs.
The capsized sky is mad
Over our mayday lives
As, brief in a butterfly
Of love we meet and die.
And so those harpies of peace
Rive and rend and destroy
The mnemonic demigod:
Those demons of what we did.

Epithalamium for Two Friends

Sweat, wicked kissers, in your stark
Hate of the whitewashed day;
By the queen-swarm of a breast
Where lolls a honeycombing hand
No peeping constellations may
Eavesdrop upon you as you clip
Each other in old Adam's nest,
And in an evening silvered cup
Love's upspringing sunrise catch
Till the winged bloodhorses of sex
Dead heat, and meet their match.

No, never lift those heavy eyes
(Like mirrors opposite they view
Two whole advancing worlds of two)

For that inspector with a sword
Outside your bedroom keeping guard
Who mistakes for a sadder place
The sacred bed and garden of
Your permissible embrace.

Across the globe from Africa
To New Zealand you have bent
The rainbow of your sacrament
And promise of a Milky Way,
Under whose nuptial arch so many
—Folk and flower, fish and beast—
Would shelter, if they only could,
From afflictions not understood,
Till half the world curled up like any
Babe against your threefold breast.

And yet your bed is full enough
When empty of all things except
Two who erect their house of love
On the dark spot where Adam wept.
But let no poison of the veins
Shake an Egyptian skeleton—
These two in one another's chains
Labouring under Helicon
Prove that who loses also gains
The love that takes a world of pains.

On a Friend's Escape from Drowning off the Norfolk Coast

Came up that cold sea at Cromer like a running grave
    Beside him as he struck
Wildly towards the shore, but the blackcapped wave
    Crossed him and swung him back,
And he saw his son digging in the castled dirt that could save.
    Then the farewell rock
Rose a last time to his eyes. As he cried out
    A pawing gag of the sea
Smothered his cry and he sank in his own shout
    Like a dying airman. Then she
Deep near her son asleep on the hourglass sand
    Was awakened by whom
Save the Fate who knew that this was the wrong time:
    And opened her eyes
On the death of her son's begetter. Up she flies
    Into the hydra-headed
Grave as he closes his life upon her who for
    Life has so richly bedded him.
But she drove through his drowning like Orpheus and tore
    Back by the hair
Her escaping bridegroom. And on the sand their son
    Stood laughing where
He was almost an orphan. Then the three lay down
    On that cold sand,
Each holding the other by a living hand.

The Death of Manolete

You, king, die. Mithra. Where was death
Hiding for those ten hours when you lay
Endowing Lenares with that great red legend?
The Monster. Dead. Drag the bright corpse away.

Did the sword shriek in his hand? The sand
Wept as he fell. You, king, die. The Miura
Groaned as he gored his god. But the long
Face of a stone and a saint only set surer

Into the calm that had always crowned it. You,
King, die. The killer with a bull's hair on his belly
Goes towering to his death under a cape.
Black that Islero honours the place where he fell.

O expiation! The king and the bull, kissing,
Enter and share a kingdom. The sword and horn
Sleep side by side. Justice. You, kings, die.
Between this man and this bull a myth is born.

Justice at Midnight

I. [*The Ballad of Wild Children*]

Down the long hall of night fly those wild children
    Conceived in a dream.
The great gales rage in the trees outside the window,
    And, curved like a scream,
The moon, for an instant visible through the tempest,
    Cries out as it drowns,
But still down the long hall of night fly those wild children
    My heart disowns.

O orphans of all blind egoes in their eyries,
    Both claw and lamb
Bleed, really, together. Double-headed the eagle
    Or vulture I am—
Dogger or digger of death. Strikes then lightning
    Through my white ceiling,
But every affection has already died, and broken
    Is every precious feeling.

With teeth of stars
In the watches of the night those huge gears wheeling
Grind up all power and all glory until
Meshed in the clock of years
Nothing remains of our spiritual pride save only
A despair of hands knocking
Like a lost idiot at the asylum of heaven
And a mocking echo.

Then the wild children who flew down the long hall of night
With tears and rain
Like fair-haired lambs frightened in violent weather
Return again
Armed from the teeth of the dragon, howling out loud
For Justice and Vengeance,
While, overhead, smiling, blood drips from the jaws
Of the heavenly engines.

II. [*Justice at Midnight*]

1.
She comes across the sobbing years
O who will give her half a bed
The blind somnambulist who hears
Every word we never said.

2.
The clock walked down the corridor,
Pronounced imperative of sin
The love, the outrage and the hour.
I heard the knock. Justice walked in.

3.
Towering the far side of the table
Tall as the pregnant midnight she
Crossed the floor, stepped from a symbol
To bring judgment home on me.

4.
Outside the Newton window I hear
Those numbers whom the gods love
Go strolling home. But I believe
Apollyon guffaws in my ear.

5.
(A bridal spring in the next room
Sends generation creaking on
Its red-handed quest to bring
Another infant prodigal home.)

6.
Then at the ceremony of this hour
All seasick anarchies of conscience
Break through the clashing doors of our
Impenitential violence.

7.
The dead brides shriek across the seas
As the floor bangs like a bed:
The brown bones clamouring in the cupboard
Burst out and axe with memories.

8.
O tidal sailing love that idly
Sleeps on a seeming summer day
The fell rock of full circle wildly
Strikes from half a world away!

9.
Groan, groan, old zanies in the floor,
I put you murderously to sleep
And when you turned and called to me
I gave you seven more to keep.

10.
I gave you seven more to keep
You cacodaemons oversexed,—
Now underground I hear you weep
Till I surrender my soul next.

11.
The long-armed midnight gazes down.
Mercy the mad mother shall cry
As Justice, gathering up her own,
Watches the mad children die.

12.
Midnight. Sweet moon upon that lake
Where, done, all loving, daily, nightly,
Sinks in reflection, let the heart break
Early as the dawn sings coldly.

13.
So up and down this ticktocking room
Those broken newborn veronicas pace
And each one with its kiss-crossed face
Need never tell me why or whom.

14.
The son is nailed on the long clock.
Justice walks in. I hear the knock.
And every death looks up with dry
Tears into my drowning eye.

15.
Justice! I cry and the wide walls
Fall in, skull caves, and the stars drop
Out of far worlds through my eyeballs,
  And all my hearts stop.

III. [The Ballad of the Three Dead and the Three Living]

Three men in a limousine
  travelling westward
Passed three men in a limousine
  travelling upward.

At the instant of crossing
  the westward three

Turned their heads and observed
  that the others were dead.

But they handled their dolls
  in the rear seats,
And they thought of the white wines
  and the sweetmeats.

They looked at their phosphorescent
  watches and flashed
Gold rings. They forgot
  questions would be asked.

The passing limousine
  in which the dead
Men sat, did not pass
  but travelling sped

Upward, stayed
  aslant the window
Like an angular nightmare.
  the three living played

With their sweet doxies.
  then together the dead
Men said in dark
  tones: Sure, we're dead,

But not so dead
  we forget the blondes
And the gin and the glittering
  automobiles.

But let us warn you:
  that can't last.
You'll soon find the gin
  as stiff as glue

And the tarts' pretty tits
  hang from the bones

So narrow and cold
  like tombstones.

But the living were deaf to
  the dead talk and did
What they always did,
  ignoring the dead.

No lorry hit them. No train
  fulfilled the speech
Of the prophetic dead.
  But the three living played

With their silent dolls
  and flashed their watches
Like jewelled prizes.
  But questions were asked.

IV. [The Caterwauling Beast at Last has Utterance]

O dove whom I never knew and shall never know,
  Open your spirit over
The unguided way I go, and at my side
  Guide me for ever.

O dove whom I never knew and shall never know,
  When I turn, seeking
The passion and grace of your presence, let me not witness
  The vision disappearing.

O dove whom I never knew and shall never know,
  Nest now on my tongue,
Pacify the speaking fires and ashes of the mouth
  And cherished ostracized wrong.

O dove whom I never knew and shall never know,
  Lean over the sad water
Of my witnessing, and from your heavenly ruling
  Prove that love is greater—

O dove whom I never knew and shall never know,
 Greater than any
Enemy. And that, in the end, your advocation is stronger
 Than men or money.

V. [Calendar Thoughts for the Month of the Dead]

Let loose the splendours of the dead.
 The howling head, the chattering bone
Ride flouncing through a living room
 And strike my heart to a stone.

O gold lamp floating in a wood
 Where it is morning dark,
Sing out and affirm the same truth as
 A rainbow and an ark.

What is that image in the sky
 Which, once having seen,
The intellect of man turns away
 And longs for what has been?

The headlines whoop about the house
 As mad as cuckoo clocks:
I have found death and degradation
 Slipped through a letter box.

No peace shall ever to the false
 And forking eye bring rest
For foul the liar in the glass
 Shall every breathing nest.

And it may be as long a day
 As any night ever was,
When seeking my true God he finds
 A liar in that glass.

Only the orthodox and huge dead
 To pluck up by the hair

The falling moral man can show
   Angels ascending there.

O sepulchre, O pinnacle
   Of holy tongue, of Mosaic tooth,
Teach the white liar that his worm
   Splits the heart of the truth.

There is no deeper shorter cut
   Than when with Geiger eyes
The wingless wonder, daring the grave,
   Dives up into mysteries.

Walk out, twelfth man, and step straight through
   The hanging fires of fate,
Or, sniggering, three old women will carry
   You through the cold gate.

For we are clipped to that Arachne
   Who will not let us cease
Until, locked hot in those cold arms,
   Her wilderness is peace.

The ocean, risen over the rocks,
   Has dispossessed the world,
But still the Seven Sorrows rock
   A cradle and a child.

VI. [A Farewell]

Those with our victory in their hands
Lift ticking to the final cloud
Those instruments with this fate endowed:
Hapless a prince in the ground
Who to the dawn of wounds has bowed
Turns once again that face to us
In whose royal hieroglyph we saw
The judgment of that fatal law
Invoking universal detritus.

O far the wall where I have stood
And seen the fighting in the air
Of such societies as give
Mercy and honey to the grave.
Move you who walk by crutch and dog
To find the city where we lay,
Move and look down upon that home
Shattered by triumphant day.
So at the double drum we stepped
And forget where a happy hill
Sleeps in our silence. She is here,
The red adulteress in the sky.
My last infirmity is life
The voices from America call,
And in its trench the dead beast wails
To speak a first and last farewell.

A Domestic Poem

Monologue of the Wife

O Love in your empty bed
Here is my harrowing.
I watch that hero stride
His sword erect and pride
As red as my own blood,
Rise up at this bedside
To haunt my solitude.
O sad the fallow places,
Where is their harrowing?
They lie so lonely now
To see the rutting plough
Driving its bridegroomed horn
Over remoter landscapes
And joy on other faces.
The smile is on their lips
To see that share so worn,

That pride in an eclipse
Its furrowing duty done.
His sceptre is abused
By arrogance of womb
His diadem is used
To ornament the crime,
While I lie empty here
Like a cold sea at dawn
Awaiting a rise of hero
His fiery striker drawn
To aggrandize my farrow
And glorify what's born.

Monologue of the Husband

How can I ever escape
So pinioned to that thigh?
I fly my horoscope
In the star of that eye,
And bound in the decrees
Babe, sacrament and rope
Of those bridal knees?
The yoked beast must quest
Far from its loved cave
And the devoted breast,
For ridden passion craves
New victims and votives.
The beast devouring flesh
Is jaded of its own—
The two that are made one,
And can only refresh
His sick and obscene machine
In those gross beds of flesh
Wherein no spirit lies
To bind the heroic beast
Down with analogies.
But the dovetailing fury
Of those two with one back,
Rages in that void orgy
From which all human glory

Of spirit or of heart
Has been thrust out. Thrust out—
O garden of a memory!—
And so the vindictive Adam
Debars from his carnal love
That tyrannic paraclete
Who from a paradise drove
Us into sexual freedom.
Thus the vindictive Adam
Avenges a lost Eden
In the unholy embrace
Of all strumpeting women.
He disgraces disgrace.
O who could ever bear
To know again in his arms
The victress of that pair
He sees now only in dreams
Of innocence foregone?
Thus this intemperate beast
Roams furiously alone
From loveless breast to breast
From cave and lair and hole—
His rod can never rest
Seeking to rack the soul—
So these sad monsters range
Over the rocks and bones
Of sexual satisfacion
To degrade the Angel
And desecrate God's vision
With a stick and two stones.
I hide my one-horned head,
That skull-capped mastodon
In the hot death of the bed
Where neither good nor bad
But a beast's toil is done.
And hissing in her spirals
The dappled temptress flenses
My skeleton of its morals
And red ram of the senses.
So in the rummaged pit

I kill the man in and out
Splayed on that proud fork.
No love, no love, no love,
O let no brightness in—
But the sheet-lightning shove
Where we end, and begin.

A Song of the Sea

And if I love you
  What's that to you?
You'll love someone else and
  I know who.

And if you love me
  What's that to me?
My heart's up the river and
  I'm at sea.

If we love one another
  All day and night,
O the liar's the one with
  His eye so bright.

For the face that you truly
  Love for ever
Is the one that you see when
  You look in the river.

And the one who loves me most
  Under the sky
Is the one with the green and
  Familiar eye.

And so O my only
  My lonely love,
We will love one another
  As long as we live.

But the world is so wide and
 The heart so small
It's a wonder that people
 Can love at all.

Down in the deep ground
 Bisexuals squirm
O if only we found it
 As easy as worms.

But the smoke like a ghost
 Rises up from the stack
And no wind O no wind
 Can gather it back.

For if I love you
 What's that to you?
I look in a mirror
 And only see you.

And if you love me
 What's that to me?
You look in a glass and
 It's me that you see.

Wild horses are tearing
 The whole world apart
So we can see that
 It's got no heart.

By water and willow
 I'll sit down and weep
For the star that can never
 Fall ever asleep

But hears in its dreams
 The blues of the sea:
"And if you love me,
 What's that to me?"

Ballad of the Muse at Sea

I lean against a lonely door
   Under a black hill.
What are the fallen feathers for
   White on the window sill?

It is the seabird of desire
   Turned into bitter salt
Come home to roost by a dead fire.
   I saw the image melt.

Once, once over the bright-eyed sea
   That pinioned symbol rose
So high there were two suns in the sky,
   And only golden seas.

The mounted dolphins of my heart
   Sprang up the fiery stairs
Into the sunrise. And never to part
   Joy went about in pairs.

I felt the mind in a great deep
   Roll like a whale possessed
Across the breeding ground of my sleep
   And break out of my breast.

Or over the placid glass of youth
   Sailed the red swan of love
And recklessly a royal path
   Down the long doldrum drove.

So lofty over rock and bar
   The young rainbow hung
I held all hazardous things that are
   Under the arch of my tongue.

Asleep in tempests of the mind
   Such halcyons lay smiling

That every affliction seemed to find
    A pearl of reconciling.

O innocence, O innocence,
    The dove falls from the sky.
O Larvae of existence,
    Vultures return on high.

This is a sad word here written
    Because it cannot speak
To the one whom I have not forgotten,
    Dead many passions back.

O white face at the dark pane,
    O wild voice in the cellar,
You cry out against a hurricane,
    You supplicate a killer.

I lean beside a lonely door
    Under a black hill.
What is that fallen image for
    White on the window sill?

Cycle of Six Lyrics

I. [*The Dove of the Sea*]

O Doves, dismember me!
Here as I hang high
At my bone broken tree
Down from the bright fury
Descend with a wild cry.
O Doves, dismember me!

Spirit of those cold seas
That first were, and shall be
Last of the universe,

Alight, alight and be
Cold comforter to me.
O Love, remember us!

II. [The Rose and the Rod]

I saw the rose and the rod
Walk hand in hand on water
The bread of the creator:
Bulrushed our cradles rode
Wherever those two had trod
Generation burned on water.

O the rod, the rod is red
I hold in my hot hand,
And cold at the bedside
A ghost rose up and cried:
I rose from the grave's end
To prove no one has died.

III. [Heroes and Worms]

The dragons of the breast
Devour and drag down
Those seraphim of the mind
Who trumpet to attest
That Destiny is our own.
What is not is best.

I, cowboy with a spear,
Transfix my own heart
To kill the worm down there
Tearing St. George apart—
But O that worm turns
Into my heart of hearts.

IV. [*Swansong of the Hyena*]

Where are those words that once
Alighted like swans upon
Our silent deserts of sense
And gave us oases?
They are all turned into stone
Like Memnon's effigies.

The rat and the hyena
Nest in my innermost
And sacred tabernacle.
I and my soul have seen
A vision of our foul ghost
And heard its mad crackle.

V. [*O Pearl and Breasted World*]

O pearl and breasted world
At whose green spring I slake
This bitterness of Ego,
And, a snivelling child,
Hush for its mother's sake,
Await my imago:

Let the natural causes
That unite us to
Our pearl and breasted mother
Exercise their forces
Till we are made to do
Justice by one another.

VI. [*Narcissus and the Star*]

I will not look within
Where at the hot pit hisses
A diet of worms and a demon
Adoring his mirror twin

More than any Narcissus
The issue of his semen.

But as the first and last
Dead suns rise and set
Over and hereafter
The sweet star and the past—
Glory without regret
For all things ever after.

II

The View from a Blind I

Poem as Dedication

How shall I ever know
with such a darkness falling
over the affectionate rivers
that from the high heart flow
under what trees they wander
holding in colder hands
those looking glass memories,
where and why they now go
the peregrines who were my friends?

I see them in the morning
of that bright time that was,
when everywhere, like a garden,
spread out its bedding grass
before our feathered feet,
and that mouth of an ass
the heart, could only harden
under the bruise and bite
of our progressive burden,
the love with which we're laden
enormous as the night.

My sister by the golden
shore of the largest sea
takes to her bosom folded
the Torrigianan children
like cherubs of the Ascension
as the true image should be,
to find in that heavenly water
of human dedication
the veronica of her daughter
gazing like a reflection
out of their golden faces
renewed upon her knee.

Or in her little cottage
pensive by Kew Green

with its pond where the cattle
    once by Hogarth seen,
now, like that local painter,
    asleep in a deeper scene,
there she, again my sister,
    under the royal linden,
lies dreaming down that vista
    that, like a tea-party garden,
fills with old friends in a mist, a
    population, a guerdon.

Rise at my other side then
    those whom no morning bell
will ever waken and call
    to walk with me again.
And perhaps most of all
    for them I now reclaim
the splendour of each soul
    and honour of each name,
not to enumerate here
    in a small house of fame
but to keep bright and warm
    all, all the same
the inextinguishable flame.

The sorrowing Daphne who changed
    no, not into a tree
but into that stone so strange
    I felt a rock's misery
and saw what so seldom before
    the heart had looked upon:
such a weeping of conscience draw
    blood out of a stone.
And the dead cry, What has sexual
    love to do with us?
And as they cry, the funeral
    flesh stands up.

Who is she, since I cannot find
    her name of nature

that naked mother confined
  to a nine month future?
No, not to her I votive give
  what she has always taken,
the spirit that knew it was alive
  simply because it's broken.
Will love personify her verb
  and make the bed a cradle
so that her pregnant sighs disturb
  the dust with its own riddle?

To those friends, therefore, whom the sea
  or the wide grave, or time
sets on the farthest shores of love
  where only memory
may lift its olive branch to them—
  to them, over the wave
on whose crowned crest the white new moon
  as faithfully as the old
has wreath and chaplet of light strewn
  renewal of its love—
to them, over death and division
  of what can never be told
I lift the laurelled hand of my affection
  and write the word in gold.

Roman Poem I

A Visit to Lake Albano

Why is this lake so sacred? It is sacred
  Because it is still.
Such a stillness is holy, for, unlike a river
  Or even the sea
Those huge mythologies endemic overhead
  May, without a lie,
Behold themselves here as they truly believe
  The gods to be.

Shown in the drowning heavens of Albano
Would they rather
Sleep in its deeper altitudes than the sky?
Sometimes a feather
From them descends onto the evening surface
To take upon
Itself the curve and veer of that faint sail
Leaning for haven
Over Albano. Or a small fish may rise
Seeking to leap
Into the mackerel patterning of their wings
And dying eyes.
Holy Albano, I have seen the low storm
Saunter more slowly
Over your font and prism, as its form
Immersed in so
Lucid a peace received a christening grace:
Or perhaps more
Slowly moved over not to vex that still face
With a dragging shower.
Birds in your air
Loiter like visiting hierophants who hope
To steal from the place
Some miraculous touch. So I, too, this day
Having further come
And for as brief a slaking at this lake
In spiritual expiation,
Having a little refreshed in your lustrations
What may be saved
Of jaded nature, I too take away
From your holy springs
The evanescent absolution of water.

Roman Poem II

A Shower in Rome

The rain flickering here on this lonely day
Over the brown roofs of Rome
Calls to my mind I am not so far away
From my own house and home.
But then I hear the old clay within me cry
Every man is in Coventry
And to the dirt his day is exiled from
Must sometime come.

The shower sweeps westward to Ostia
Like a plane trailing
A trembling net of rain, and on the far
Landscape toiling
Armies of cloud climb and fall and are
Gone. At once the air
Sunbursts with radiance like a shattered ceiling
Dazzling everywhere.

Everywhere save here in the vaults of the heart
Where no sun can
Delve to the bloodstained urn—so dark a part
Of the unhouselled man
That only a gnashing of death can penetrate
From all those also immured
In the life long home. Interred in its fate
Bone howls to be heard.

But nevertheless above, like birds with rain,
The hands of circumstance
Unwind my blinding sheets and, once again
I feel the spirit dance
Up from its unholy cave, and regain
That illumination once
Unhaunted by the bell and clappered presence
Of human degradation.

Down in its pits the triumph of the Tarquin
    Regales those smiling dead
Just as though human delight could win
    Life instead
Back from the damp tomb and the last bed.
    Sexual joy within
These muddy tenements lifts up its head
    To begin, for ever, again.

And caged in rock beside the Capitol
    Padding her twenty foot track
The mother of Rome, loping up and back,
    Smiles as the kids howl
Proudly: Lupe! at that imperial
    Bitch on the prowl—
The pride of a creature that has never died
    Crowns her, and her whole pack.

A bed of roses and a wreath of bay
    Birds of a shower, bear
Down to these tarnished demigods of clay—
    Triumph is here
To aggrandise with the trophies and regalia
    Of our crossed victories,
Or to degrade, as with a snivelling shower,
    The Æenean glories.

Roman Poem III

A Sparrow's Feather

There was this empty birdcage in the garden.
    And in it, to amuse myself, I had hung
pseudo-Oriental birds constructed of
    glass and tin bits and paper, that squeaked sadly
as the wind sometimes disturbed them. Suspended
    in melancholy disillusion they sang

of things that had never happened, and never
    could in that cage of artificial existence.
The twittering of these instruments lamenting
    their absent lives resembled threnodies
torn from a falling harp, till the cage filled with
    engineered regret like moonshining cobwebs
as these constructions grieved over not existing.
    The children fed them with flowers. A sudden gust
and without sound lifelessly one would die
    scattered in scraps like debris. The wire doors
always hung open, against their improbable
    transfiguration into, say, chaffinches
or even more colourful birds. Myself I found
    the whole game charming, let alone the children.
And then, one morning—I do not record a
    matter of cosmic proportions, I assure you,
not an event to flutter the Volscian dovecotes—
    there, askew among those constructed images
like a lost soul electing to die in Rome,
    its feverish eye transfixed, both wings fractured,
lay—I assure you, Catullus—a young sparrow.
    Not long for this world, so heavily breathing
one might have supposed this cage his destination
    after labouring past seas and holy skies
whence, death not being known there, he had flown.
    Of course, there was nothing to do. The children
brought breadcrumbs, brought water, brought tears in their
    eyes perhaps to restore him, that shivering panic
of useless feathers, that tongue-tied little gossip,
    that lying flyer. So there, among its gods
that moaned and whistled in a little wind,
    flapping their paper anatomies like windmills,
wheeling and bowing dutifully to the
    divine intervention of a child's forefinger,
there, at rest and at peace among its monstrous
    idols, the little bird died. And, for my part,
I hope the whole unimportant affair is
    quickly forgotten. The analogies are too trite

I Walked by a Window in Ireland

For Patrick Swift

I walked by a window in Ireland
When it was Christmas evening
And a long dark rain was falling.
I heard some fishermen singing
A rant of the old days gone
Down and the seadogs drowning.
I heard the bird of the morning
Cry out at a wrong time
And was it the word of a warning
He cried—was it the same
Dark long rain of a crime
I felt at my sinnermost heart
Against this Christian time?
The dead men walk the streets
And do not know they are me:
You are the seadog that stalks
My blood hound up from the sea.
And arm in arm we go strolling
From house to house and from
Locked door to barred door
Knocking at every home
And ask at each one for
A hand through the bolted door
A heart through the latched breast
And a little love in the hand
To let our spirits rest.
Not at that Christian time
A dead dog and I received
Not a hard board, not bread
At any outstretched hand,
Not on that Christless evening
The living or the dead
Were listened to, nor loved,
Were neither seen nor received.
And the bird of warning sang on

As if its breast was broken,
For never a loving word
Have we ever really heard,
Or ever spoken.

True Love, True Love, what have I done?

True love, true love, what have I done
  That I can find no rest?
Only the breaking of this bed rock
  Nightlong in my breast.

True love, true love, what have I done
  To drive such a scissoring wind
Over the seas of my sleep like
  A harpy of the mind?

True love, true love, what have I done
  That, wherever I go,
I walk upon that sobbing fossil—
  Eros in the snow.

True love, true love, what have I done?
  —So violent a thing
That every wind and word a witness
  Against my breath will bring?

True love, true love, what have I done
  Save watch it sail away
That gold haired shell with Aphrodite
  Nailed to a prow of clay?

True love, true love, what have I done?
  O never and never return!
I have seen the lightning whip the shrouds
  And watched the mermaids burn.

True love, true love, what have I done
    That I can find no rest?
The wormwood head, the gilded image
    Sink weeping in the west.

True love, true love, what have I done?
    In assuaging sea
I drown, but still the fishes whisper
    Love without end to me.

Circular from America

Against the eagled
Hemisphere
I lean my eager
Editorial ear
And what the devil
You think I hear?
I hear the Beat
No not of the heart
But the dull pulpitation
Of the New Art
As, on the dead tread
Mill of no mind,
It follows its leaders
Unbeaten behind.
O Kerouac Kerouac
What on earth shall we do
If a single Idea
Ever gets through?
The English have seventy
Gods and no sauce
(The French have Voltaire
And Two Maggots of course)

But ½ an idea
To a hundred pages
Now Jack, dear Jack,
That ain't fair wages
For labouring through
Prose that takes ages
Just to announce
That Gods and Men
Ought all to study
The Book of Zen.
If you really think
So low of the soul
Why don't you write
On a toilet roll?
And as for Rextroh
That angry king
He'd court anyone
Or any thing.
If you pick your judgements
Up in the street
Why be so bloody
Indiscreet
As to display 'em
Like a dirty sheet?
O pen is alive
I beg you tell 'em
What wouldn't we give
For some cerebellum?
Whole chapters and verses
Of bric-à-brac
Will bring Carlos Williams
And not a dove back.
'I first met Dean
Not long after my wife
And I split up.'*
Gawd, what a life.
I'm a Dharma Bum.
Gawd, I'm a toad.

* The opening of *On the Road*.

I'm wide. I'm out.
I'm off the Road.
But on Third Avenue
(Like Rome only more so
A street as gregarious
As any Corso)*
The shady bars
Open at morning
Like nenuphars
And the Beats yawn in
From their motor cars.
O its early to bed
You story tellers
If you're not on Fulbrights
Or Rockefellers
And only the blondes
In their skin tight jeans
Are living on private
Or public means.
Whaddya want?
A spade?† A fink?‡
Don't goof, cripple.
Man, I stink.
And the silver towers
Of vanity sink
Into the golden
Seas of drink,
And round and round
At the fiery brink
Fly those who do every
Thing but think.
And all the while
From Maine to Utah
The virgins arrive
On foot and scooter
With bags that will never
Again be neuter.
Yes, far away

* Gregory Corso, author of *Gasoline*. † Negro. ‡ Homosexual.

On the other side
Of the Middle Worst
And the Great Divide
There, there on the gilded
Coasts of the West
The Great I Am's
Are the happiest
For somewhere in Yonkers
They're shocking amoeba
With a cyclotron
Or the Queen of Sheba.
O beautiful
America
I have a feeling
I've come too far—
Did the plane put down
On the right star?
O tell me where the Statue
Of Libertines is
In the middle of Erewhon
Or Atlantis?
And the dead whores glitter
In Central Park
Just before every
Thing goes dark.
Down in the Village
The parvenu
Dreams of Madison
Avenue
And on Madison
The copywriters
Dream of the calm
Nights of St. Vitus
As in the arms
Of their advertisers
They gollop down
Their tranquillisers;
And the workmen burrowing
Into the sidewalk
('Dig we must

For growing New York')*
Chaw ten-inch cigars
As they work,
And dogs and children
On long lists
Attend their psycho
Analysts.
The automobiles
As large as whales
Sweep up and down
Like hearses. Tales
Of Offmen softly
Echo over
Streets choked up with
Four leafed clover,
Yet oh us lucky
Eleven million
Would give it all
To be one simple
Nice Sicilian.

And, every week,
Like a public crime
We sit in our toilets
Glued to the slime
Of the last issue
Of a loose Time.
And high on their pinnacles
The Committees sit
Denouncing all sanity
In the name of God
And unanimity.
And the ghost of a great
Democratic conception
Shrieks out: 'I confess
To a little deception
But I meant well
Make me an exception.'

* Stencilled on all roadmenders' trestles.

O Gawd once again
I hear the beat
Of the rock and rolling
Paraclete:
Man, you know
Our attitude
Ain't a defeat,
It's a beatitude.
We all mean well,
Yeah, we all mean well
Like the Esso pipeline
That goes to hell.
For brother, brother,
The Am Express
Has illegalised
Human distress
And in the end
All our ills
Succumb to a bottle
Of vitamin pills
And the logic of
The formal mind
Acknowledge it's super
Annuated
By IBM
Incorporated.
Till the voice of the Turtle
Or the New Yorker
Intones the verses
Of Garcia Lorca:
'The jungle of To-morrow.
Ah, that's it, man
All caught up in
The beard of Whitman.'
And 'Enough!' enunciates
The Spectre of James
'Don't spare the horses.
Throw out the dames.
Just drive like mad
Straight through the flames

And we'll all take tea
At the Court of St. James.
The pyrotechnics
Of shall I say Hell
Have reached Minneapolis
And St. Paul as well:
So lower the curtain
At all the borders
And close my books
Until further orders.'

Two Poems for Painters

I. [*To Kit Barker*]

Where high upon his sighing hill
My brother, with the Fates at bay,
Stands as if contemplating all
The sweating climbers of the day,
But cool at noon upon them they
Shall feel the light and loving fall
Of his abstracted sympathy
And this commiseration shall
Seem to us like a cupful of the sky.

Where high upon his sighing hill
He rests a hard and sunrise hand
Still visages of avalanche will
Haunt him with all hazard till
Trapped among catastrophes
And hounded by Medusa down,
Knife in hand he crops those painted trophies
As noble as his own
Gentle head, sacrificed eye, and his heavy crown.

II. [To Francis Bacon]

Now the torn spectre leers forward through rain
And the dog howls
Pity for all things, may this lightning nerve
Nailed to the clouds
Keep half a nightmare leaping in the darkness
Until it claims
The floodlight of human agony in these great frames
And the brush screams
As his wronged hand lifts it towards such crimes

When he was lost in the gas-filled chambers of spirit
How did he find a way?
Like the eddying squid. He roams the bed of our fathoms
And his sunken searchlights play
Over illusions until they
Cross on that torn undersea ghost and illumine a face
Death has already devoured.

The Ballad of Yucca Flats

I saw four horsemen riding
Up from the dawn of day.
'O no, there's no more living
For ever in Nevada.'

I heard the first horseman singing
As he rode on his way:
'Everyone begins to die
Outward from Nevada.'

I saw the second horseman
Lift up his head and say:
'No, there's nowhere left to hide
In all the sands of Nevada.'

And the third horseman looked down
At his red hand of clay:
'O amigos, we've come full circle
In the sands of Nevada.'

But the fourth horseman stood up
Silent in his stirrups
Till he saw in the morning sky
The rose of Apocalypse.

. . .

Then the four horsemen dropped
Down into Death Valley
Where the sun flogs the rocks
Till the sand runs bloody.

And the air there turns to salt
And the salt to gravel,
And only that bird overhead
Knows the way to travel.

There the four boney horsemen
With nothing at all in their bags
Pulled up their palominoes
And stretched out their dusty legs.

And the brittle lizards scooted
Among the brimstone rocks
And the gilah monsters watched them
With eyes like little clocks.

Then as they sat there dealing
A hand at the twenty one
Out from his belt the first horseman
Slipped his Mexican gun:

'Amigos O amigos
I think I'm through,' he cried
'They'll know that Death Valley
Was the place where I died.'

As the suicide bullet drove like
A horn through his head
He saw the dawn of wrath load
Time with a grain of lead.

And as he lay a-dying
Cold clay on cold day
He whispers: 'I wish to Christ that
He never made Nevada.'

So with rocks they covered him
And left him like ashes there.
And on they went, the one with two,
Over the back of Nowhere.

. . .

Next evening as they bivouacked
Under the summer moon
The second horseman spoke: 'I saw
Himself this afternoon.

And I feel a kind of empty
Space here at my side
Just as though Death Valley
Burned underneath my hide.

It's the red, red rose of the desert
That marks my parting day,
O for ever blows that dead rose
That grows in Nevada!'

And he lay down under the Dogstar
Never again to wake
And the rocks around him heard his heart
Like a rock within him break.

Then the last two threw their saddles
Over the stallion backs
And into the west, under the moon,
Rode on their one way tracks.

. . .

Nevada deathwatch Nevada
Your silver stars look down
And shiver as tomorrow
Triggers a redder dawn.

Then the two horsemen heard the
Terrible train on high
As the engines of Nevada
Rocked the entire sky.

The fourth horseman turned his
Cold gaze from the West:
'This is the place for you, Jack.
This is the spot to rest.'

They lay their skulls on the saddles,
Their bones on the saddle mats,
Till morning, like an exploding rose,
Burst over Yucca Flats.

Still the Angel of Death, that fourth horseman,
Glared from his dead eye:
'Jack,' says he, 'so now you know
It ain't so hard to die.'

'It ain't so hard to die, Jack,
And every mother's son
One day will sleep beside you here
When all is sad and done.'

'So haunt the westering desert, Jack,
Haunt it like mirages,
And whisper to Los Alamos
I pay the wages.'

Then that immortal horseman
Smiled and rode away.
'There's never a day,' quoth he, 'but dawns
Redder in Nevada.'

A Little Song in Assisi

Sprightly the cockcrowing
sun from that stone bed
high in the hilly morning
where a saint lay down his head
steps gallivanting.

All small things including
bird lizard and beast
and the dayspring beginning
dance from the doors of the east
like lambs skedaddling.

There is such an alighting
tenderness in the air
like wings after hovering
that a dove might be here,
hidden but apprehending.

Peasant and priest toiling
over the patched hill side,
the acolyte at his hoeing,
see from that iron tressel
the saint's huge brother rising

until, like a lark, lifting
the valleyed Umbrian veils,
the heart of Francis, dazzling
bird in the air, reveals
the grace of that ragged man
transfiguring everywhere.

Variation on Swans

To Dom Moraes

I.

When from the west of darkling Luss
    I saw one glaring swan
Ride through the arches of the mist
    And, like a death, glide on:

Then rain assailed the evening, and
    The water twittered, like
A hundred thousand crowsfeet on
    The surface of the lake.

The little church against the hill
    With a twisted tree beside it—
On six bright strokes that spellbound world
    Like a dead sea divided.

Three islets in looped chains of cloud
    Hung, and the moon slowly
Lifted her huge breast to the lake
   And made the water holy.

A solitary swinging bird
    Stirred by the six stroke bell
Cried once above the lake, and then
    Again the silence fell.

Variation on Swans

II.

O darkling valley of the Usk
    There I would wish to be
With the wild swan glimmering in the dusk
    As though to haunt me.

O darkling valley of the Usk
  Those kingfisher days are gone
And only derelict echoes hiss
  The whisper of the swan.

O darkling valley of the Usk
  Whenever the rain descends
Will your dimmed waters mirror less
  The faces of my friends?

O darkling valley of the Usk
  What bright shadows remain
To wander by those banks where we
  Will never walk again?

Then from the west of darkling Usk
  I saw the glaring swan
Ride through the arches of the mist
  And, like a death, glide on.

Nine Beatitudes to Denver

I.

From the left handed administrations of ghouls with skeleton keys
From the postman, the seven sworded shepherd and the kings
  of Switzerland
From the glory of the Marine Corps and the charters of religious
  institutions
From the dog, from the four dugged Cadillac and from an empire
  of stenographers
O heavenly telegram, O word without mercy, preserve us!

I shall be happy to disclose why angels detest Museums
And why the fish of the sea rejected Democracy
Why engineers never inaugurate revolutions
And why those who weep by the deathbed of Alexander shall
  inherit nothing.

I prefer, however, to retain the conditional silence of words
And intend to conceal my meaning within the mystery provided
for that purpose;
I mean the poem whose pleasure it is to remove her six veils
In order to display the straitjacket in which she performs her dance
before the altar.

See, I have nothing to conceal save the city of London burning
at my breast
And a long line of assassins and sharp practisers hiding in
my right eye.
To the laws of human communication I propose to apply
a blow torch:
Is it really worth while to force one's best friends into suicide?

From the ribald advances of queens and those medals awarded
for charities
From the drums of middleclass regiments and the Pegasi of
Mobilgas
From all houses with three exits and those women who have none
O you on the far side of the wall, eternally preserve us!

II.

There were, of course, those occasions when armies held dances
When heroic festivals and the balls of Hercules attracted
much admiration:
Whoever heard of the military without an expensive mess?
But it all came to nothing. The dead men declined the dance.

And so, Achilles, I provide a tent for your contumacy.
Join me here where we spend all day long signing protestations
And all night long dissembling the fear that heaven will
take no notice.
No, neither heaven nor the Bureau of Psychological Statistics.

It is perfectly natural for lovers to resent the advances
Of bacteriology, chemistry, and the Science of Substitutions.
After all, why should they waste their time sweating that labour
So much more efficiently performed by an equation?

When two statistics kiss, the experience is viable?
At the copulation of engines all the archangels tremble.
And when the heroic machine weeps at Thermopylae
Why does it mourn? The great god, man, is dead.

III.

What poet hitherto has been called upon to celebrate
The sudden departure of eight hundred pounds avoirdupois
from the sphere
Of terrestrial mechanics into the arms of a Goddess?
Will Selene appreciate impregnation by that germless ball?

I cannot persuade myself that this interstellar violation
Of a lady whom hitherto we had all thought extremely gracious
—After all, she has presided over several rather heavenly
ceremonies—
It strikes me as, well, the height of erotic presumption.
Suppose she prefers the attentions of Mars or the respectable
ring of Saturn?

Anyhow, this is no time for recrimination.
Let us enter the heavenly bedroom as circumspectly as possible.
Glass helmet, antennae, rubber penis, no contraceptives—
Who knows, after all, what the sexual tastes of a Goddess might be?

IV.

How on earth, Sausalito, shall we ever understand one another?
Inheriting, as I do, the morals of Talleyrand and the ethics
of Wallenstein
Can I ever truly comprehend the essential cynicism
Of a society invented by beach boys and supported by girls
without girdles?
What does one do in Paradise? Remove one's ivy?

I ask you, San Antonio, precisely how would one address
Zinghis? And with what salutations receive the Grand Duke
of Tuscany?

Does one offer some tea* to Li Po? And to Timor
A hank of raw bone and a skull half full of cold blood?
Or, conversely, a copy of Contact and a handshake
With a lace glove full of snot? On Russian Hill
As the Gadarene swine career down to the Pacific
Does one help them along with whips or cast a few pearl
among them?
What, my dear friend, is the Venetian thing to do?

But no. The Bacchanalian, the Dionysian, the truly
Californian Orgies come out of a nearer Orient.
The Fourteen Stations of the Beatitude to Denver,
Are these, San Bernadino, the very best we can do?
Why not crucify Rexroth, and force him to be a god?

I place my hand on my privation and elevate my cup to you,
San Jacinto,
For the temerity with which you face the rigours and terrors
Of the Golden Coast, and the bitter spiritual wilderness
Of absolute political irresponsibility.
After all, think of those Sybarites in Cochin-China.

V.

This is not, I know, the place for private revelations.
Few things are harder than to make love on paper.
And yet, Sophonisba, when I mislaid my female in Memphis
How could I ever have known such a Thais would succeed her?

No man could ever resist your collection of long playing records
And that knot you tie in your hair, why, even a horse would envy it.
The alacrity with which you leap between sheets, buttocks akimbo,
What ballerina could equal? I kiss your mouth like a gas ring.

What inspired you, Sophonisba, to lacquer your nipples black?
Nor have I ever before encountered a woman who knew
That because her sex was glass, she could only make love to a duster.
I count myself fortunate in your democratic orifices.

* Marijuana: Californian vernacular

VI.

I regret nothing, my dear girl, so much as my ability
To detect sense in all kinds of curious anachronisms like Love,
Honour and the institution of the more or less happy family.
Why do you prefer a pad when your seat is so supremely generous?

I know, Sophonisba, that the Orient is above all things mysterious
And that the great sages of Asia, the gods of the Lower Kingdom,
Could, if they would, instruct us in many things
Of which we are wholly ignorant. But why,
Why must I grow the nail of my little finger five inches longer?
Come, smother me to death with information—straight from
those open and unparallelable lips.

VII.

Imagine, my dear fellow, the fluttering of the dovecotes from
Isphahan to Lisbon, from London to Constantinople,
When the last tremendous pronunciamento issues from Venice
(West) California.
Have you any idea how many cats we address?

But, seriously, who could ever have supposed that the Great
Panjandrum and the Presidents of Assurance Corporations,
Assistant Secretaries of Literary Societies and even Universal
Profossils
Would, in so short a time, have acknowledged the existence
Of an idea whose central proposition is, simply, to love?

For generations and generations the creature has been doing its best
To love the man—and the woman—next door. And now,
Now we have found out a way. It is perfectly simple.
You just go to pot together in the name of man.

It is better to lie together than to tell the truth apart.
The boy who masturbates in a public lavatory redeems
The misery of the loveless world, for one moment.
I know of no law against the island of Lesbos.
Who wants to protect his daughter from the Priapic tortoise?

Hanged in the arms of Ygdrasil, that unfriendly tree,
There is no man who would not change places with Casanova.
What bleeding woman, nailed out on the red bed of destiny
Would hesitate, my dear man, to exchange it for yours?
Yes, Love is preferable to the dictations of Fate.

VIII.

Behold, Walter Ruether, the flowering of the thousand-feathered
  Lyre-Bird
Blossoming like a giant weed* in the allotments of the West.
The cherubim of the present ride trumpeting on a cloud
Of Loatzean tea. My God, Sophonisba,
Where the hell is the roadmap to Pandemonium?

Acquainted with whole histories of Oblomov and ages of grief,
Why, my dear boy, my expensive girl, look backward
To the clay footed demigods with voices like castrati,
To the boring dead who are now no better than asphalt?
No, let us go to the park and hear what the chairs are saying.

IX.

And so, Sophonisba, I lift my short arm to you in a first valediction.
Will you remember the red nights under that Golden Gate
And the sensitive evenings given to gratifying the senses
Like a pair of spies exchanging their disguises?
Reality dare not enter the bedroom of lovers.

And when reality enters the head of the poet
Have you any idea what happens? I shall inform you.
It is transfigured into a huge stone statue
That stands and weeps for what it can never forget.
The poet persuades the past to placate its conscience.

This confession, my dear, is never, never completed.
To Ginsberg reality has, for a longwinded moment,
Broken down, howled, and shown her disconsolate heart.

* Marijuana: Californian vernacular

It is much to his honour that he has not attempted
To edit her real hysteria. Or his own.

The same ark floats on the same blood-rimmed sea.
The consequences of what we have done still wear mourning.
The red breast is shot. The ball is castrated. The clock
Wings like a bald headed eagle into the West.
I suggest, my dear friend, that, arm in arm for a moment,
We stroll through the night.

Battle Hymn of the New Republic

When the guns begin to rattle
And the men to die
Does the Goddess of the Battle
Smile or sigh?

When a hundred thousand bodies
Stink of it
Then O then the smiling Goddess
Sighs a bit.

When the dust upon those bodies
Starts to settle
Then O then the sighing Goddess
Smiles a little.

Elegy for David Gray, 1838–1860

> 'In him, as in Keats and as in another youth of genius, whose name, but the other day unheard of, Lord Houghton has so gracefully written into the history of English poetry,—David Gray—the temperament, the talent itself, is deeply influenced by their mysterious malady; the temperament is *devouring*; it uses vital power too hard and too fast, paying the penalty in long hours of utter exhaustion and in premature death.'—MATTHEW ARNOLD: *Maurice de Guérin.*

i.

But there was always a No in what he said.
    The early bird, rising,
Inscribed upon sky the mayfly breath of the dead.
    And this child, raising
The dreaming ashburnham tree of his auburn head
    Cried from Kelvingrove:
Summon the memory of what I have not said
    Here to my grave.

ii.

It was that laurelled Medusa split my tongue
    But the blinded bird
Uttering the unconditional splendour of the young
    Screamed a single word,
And she with her skulls and hideous trophies strewn
    In the echoing cave
Heard Destiny's crystal crack like a glass at a stone
    And never forgave.

iii.

And this skinny boy from Murkland stood in his long
    Pride like a striking
Adder and hissed: No! when, humming their obvious song
    The sirens came, sighing
    Of those who had once
Bartered their lives for the immortal feather
    Like singing swans:
'Let those who propose to fly pray for fine weather.'

iv.

Till the kindly shade of Arnold the Inspector
    At that bedside
Leaned over and looked down like a loving doctor
    At a suicide.
Now here, and so much later, on that lonely
    Stone with no name
I hang this verse, and this verse is the only
    Funeral game.

The Fiery Beds of Flesh

Underneath their tolling death
    In each other's arms
They lay and rolled the night away
    In each other's arms.

'I had not thought so blown and hot
    The beds of flesh could be,
Or that the stone and charnel ground
    The beds of flesh could be.'

'Ah, here,' he cried, 'here at my side
    I feel the cold finger worm,
Here like a bride, here at my heart
    I feel the cold finger worm.'

'Alone, alone, I had not known
    The fiery flesh,' she sang,
'Chant on the throne and furnace of
    The fiery flesh' she sang.

'Yet here, instead, at this hot bed
    I feel the third cold hand
At my breast laid, here at my heart
    I feel the third cold hand.'

They gazed with carrion eyes, and sighs
    Across the fiery bed
But like a prize that snake-head shone
    Across the fiery bed.

'Lie long, lie deep,' they heard it weep,
    'As you lie breast to breast.
No time to sleep in the dance of death
    As you lie breast to breast.'

'The clocks will strike, the cocks will shriek,
    Still you will never wake.
Not if the world like a babe cried out,
    Still you will never wake.'

Underneath that silent earth
    With never a word said
They lay beneath that violent oath
    With never a word said.

Not the bright horn or the dark storm
    Shall ever stir these bones.
Only the worm, the fingering worm
    Shall ever stir these bones.

Scottish Bards and an English Reviewer

To Dr. John McNeill

And in the Abbotsford
Like gabbing asses
They scale the heights
Of Ben-Parnassus
And on each shoulder
Like a rowan
A chip that goes on
Growing growing

Till every motion
Of the mind
(Not all originate
Behind)
Looks like rags
Blown amiss
Into the branches
Of prejudice.
The dark and feral
Gaelic fancy
Mysterious
As necromancy
Calling up from
Past and present
Nothing that is
Very pleasant,
And over all
The tragic scene
Of what is not
And what has been,
The cannibalistic
Sawney Bean
Stands chewing on
An arm or leg
Or sucking a testicle
Like an egg.
And strutting up and
Down the Mile
The uncrowned Laird
Of Scottish style
—Is it a Scott
He's walking with?—
The only kilted
Kiwi—Smith.
There's a Lindsay this
And a Lindsay that
There's a Craig tit
And a Craig tat
There's a Robert Tweedle
And a Robert Tum

And a Campbell looking
A bit glum
—They are all there
Chests stuck out
Pouring down gallons
Of Irish stout
And with the whiskey
Flowing free
Damning the Sassanach
Lickpenny.
'Why dinna ye
Lairn frae us?
Canna ye see
We're marvellous?
Without so much as
One word written
We're the finest poets
In all Britain.
Stand me a pint
O the singing stuff
An' I'll shoot ye an epic straight
Off me cuff.
Och, if only I still had
Me little knife
I'd cut us off at
The Forth of Fife
Or maybe I mean
The Fife of Forth
Weel, dinna fash;
Anywhere north
Of the bluidy border
That's atween
All Scottish order
And Putney Green.'
And Time draws on
And Time draws near
As we drown ten beers
In some more beer,
Till in the dim
Illumination

Of alcoholic
Stimulation
We see that all
The woes of the Scot
Ensue from God knows
Only what
But definitely
They do not
Arise from any
Fault at all
Native north of
The Roman Wall.
The minstrels flash
The witty claymore
And we all mean less
As we all say more
Till the bards sink
In a tartan clamour
Like their heroes under
The auction hammer
But from the floor
Where they lie in rows
Arises the story
Of Scotland's woes
As the voice of the bard
Sighs out of its cup:
'Why the hell dinna ye
Help me up?'
O Caledonia
Fair and wild
Bitter as bitter
Mild as mild
But the blood of a Scot
When he's had a dram
Couldn't be stopped
By Boulder Dam
So it's out o' me way
Ye lesser species
I say what I think o' ye
In me faeces.

Where O where
Would this whole warruld be
If it wasn't for Robbie
Burns and me?'
Then the stars spey out
Over Princes Street
And not one of us left
On his own feet
As we float away
Down the Royal Mile
Swearing in rime
Swabbed in style
And proud as MacPunch
All the while—
Till faintly as
We disappear
A Grieving Pibroch
Assails my ear:
'I tell you, mon,
This universe
Will go on getting
Worse and worse
Till they pass a law
That only [*sic*] Scotch
Is allowed to think
Or wear a watch
Or take a drink.
For every other
Earthly nation
Can tell the time
From their subjugation
And as for ratio
-cination,
Why, any fool who's
Not too cliquey
Knows it started
In Auld Reekie,
And every other
Heathen knows
A thristle (Scottish)

Outsings a rose.'
'And still an' all
And all the same'
Soloes the lyre o'
Jock S. Graham
'Now Dylan's dead an'
I survive,
Why, mon, I'm the only
Scald alive.'
Then the moon, like the truth,
Rose over the fog
Of the tartan night,
And sick as a dog
I made my way
To a sottish bed
And a Scottish day.

The Maidenhair Vessel with the Cradling Chain

O misted woods hanging on a hill
Under a dirty sky of those November
Evenings when only streams are not still
And even autumn knows that it is sombre
And images like reflected faces fill
The welling memory, I know I shall remember
Your evergreen aviaries of the past until
I add my lineage to your sacred number.

Then no farewell was that last image of
My trudging love that I her hunter had
With her hair tossed and tawny, and the courage of
Those who foresee defeat and are not sad,
I saw her traipsing down the evening
Track with a glass milk jug caught in her arms,
But never again shall all my believing
Even in a dream ever bring her back.

O dove, my milk and honey love, what mist
Came down and hid you from me for ever after,
With that glass pearled in your hand, and the honey kissed
Into the curl of your combs, and your small laughter
Like the waltzing of watered light? What beast
Stepped from behind a bush and dragged down
Your gathering-love-in-a-mist face to its breast
Smothering in rage what it could never own?

Into that empty house, whence you have so
Improvidently taken a last leave
I again turn in the evening, but find no
Echo of your possession or your love.
What walls could ever imitate your dove
Calling in silence from its amorous cage?
What eavesdropping shadow ever shift or move
So near as the whispering icon of your face?

Was it the unicorn of my long horned pride
Crushed your lost milkmaid underneath that hill?
I had not thought that any beast could kill
Such innocence of spirit, but would ride
Roughshod as through a morning of blue May
And not leave a hoofmark upon the day.
Now I have seen a butchered dawn lie still
Where it was broken by the brute I ride.

But these sad monsters weep beside the streams
Their elephantine vanity has ploughed up:
The heart of the tyrant is scored with his crimes;
Not every bridegroom knows when the ball should stop
And let a couple rest. I loved too much
The maidenhair vessel with the cradling chain,
And capturing it in that berserker clutch

Shattered what no remorse could restore again.
There is no shame and no pity; only regret
That innocence must either alter or die.
And mercifully the evening can forget
Its morning glories. Who could blame the high

Sun because it burns a dawn into noon,
Or dolls the midday bird with hanging veils
In the lascivious evening? But, too soon,
Harried a pearl into a hunter's moon.

Only the whole world now turns between us
My unreturning dove. Only the whole
Unholy world, and nothing, nothing more.
Hesper is not nearer now to Venus
Than I to you where you flitter alone
By a vast sea, on a dark shore.
It is not very far from pole to pole—not very far
They marry at the middle of the star.

The View from a Blind I

Written at Hadrian's Villa

From villa'd Tivoli
I look down over the plain
But like the view from a blind
Eye what I see is void.
Where once the Emperor
Mused in his alabaster
Court in a pool like a wheel
Saw he, perhaps, the same
Void in that psychic water?
Over the Campagna
As far as I can see
The farms flourish like flowers
And the confident olive
Whispers how civilized
Man and landscape can be.
Little rivers assure
The farmer of his reward
And a cynical Horace smiles
From a neat hillside that looks

Exactly like one of his odes.
O fountains of Tivoli
May crystal a single drop of
Your ostentatious torrents
Commemorate for one moment
—Flash in the sun and fade—
As bright a word as mine, then
On fostering laurel fall.
Over these gifted fields
The eye like a swift chases
Sporting among low eaves
Or skimming with lidded wings
An ariose Aniane.
As all these waterfalls
Render their copious
And votive offices
To this rivering valley
So, generous in their turn,
Seem all things here. Children
Bang and shout in the square
As ceaselessly as the fountains
Around them play. And high
Over it all the sun
Gazes like Hadrian.
And yet my blinded eye
Imposes upon the scene
A population of ruin,
The fallen pillar, the arch
Invested with poisonous ivy,
And from these vandalled tombs
Only the lizard like
A cicatrice shoots as I pass. Huge
As the sepulchre of a god
As degraded and as foregone,
Stranded in the wrong time
The Emperor's palace decays
Like ruins of the human spirit
Peopled with arthropods. So
Loud the Vox Populi
Echoes in these vast cells

As only valerian now
Rules where Hadrian reigned.
O how can the eye be so blind
As to look down upon those
Farms so fecund, so genial
With their windfalling gifts
Of what is at heart so wholly
Given to all that is good:
That true godsend, the source
Of generosity in man—
How can a neurotic I
Contemplate from its false
Altitude of self contempt
Such a prospect of truly
Holy Nature, and read
Its own faults into Eden?
Under the heavenly sun
The boys are simply at play.
Do fountains hesitate
To offer their perpetual
And charitable oblations?
Her husbanding generations.
The olive is liberal over
Not the broken Imperial pillar
With its gilt and faded laurel
Fallen, and only the snapdragon
Shuttling in its shade,
No, is not the last image and
Iconoclasm of our
Defiled and yet viable spirit.
The Roman Campagna
Covers with vines those bones
Whose great heart and soul
We have inherited,
As out of our living veins
And dying energies
Out of the shouting child
And our stony hearted I
The fountains of generation
Arise again and sing.

III

Dog, Dog in My Manger

Dog, dog in my manger, drag at my heathen
Heart where the swearing smoke of Love
Goes up as I give everything to the blaze.
Drag at my fires, dog, drag at my altars
Where Aztec I over my tabernacle raise
The Absalom assassination I my murder.

Dog, drag off the gifts too much I load
My life as wishing tree too heavy with:
And, dog, guide you my stray down quiet roads
Where peace is—be my engine of myth
That, dog, so drags me down my time
Sooner I shall rest from my overload.

Dog, is my shake when I come from water,
The cataract of my days, as red as danger?
O my joy has jaws that seize in fangs
The gift and hand of love always I sought for.
They come to me with kingdoms for my paucity—
Dog, why is my tooth red with their charity?

Mourn, dog, mourn over me where I lie
Not dead but spinning on the pinpoint hazard,
The fiftieth angel. Bay, bay in the blizzard
That brings a tear to my snowman's eye
And buries us all in what we most treasured.
Dog, why do we die so often before we die?

Dog, good dog, trick do and make me take
Calmly the consciousness of the crime
Born in the blood simply because we are here.
Your father burns for his father's sake,
So will a son burn in a further time
Under the bush of joy you planted here.

Dog, dog, your bone I am, who tear my life
Tatterdemalion from me. From you I have no peace,

No life at all unless you break my bone,
No bed unless I sleep upon my grief
That without you we are too much alone,
No peace until no peace is a happy home:
O dog my god, how can I cease to praise!

Memorial Stanzas for Louis MacNeice

I.
No, I never saw eye to eye
With this dead Irishman:
That face of a handsome sheep
Like all the mackintoshed clan
Seemed as though half asleep
Until the drinking began:
But somehow he managed to keep
His hands and his soul clean.

II.
But what can I now hold
Against this Orangeman whom
No saint ever consoled,
To whom no martyrdom
Even remotely appealed,
And whose sense of freedom
Moved only in the controlled
Ironies of our doom?

III.
And then, by accident,
We met and drank together
And I saw what was meant
By lyres of a feather:
I saw the reticent
Nature that was either
Too tender or intent
Or disguised as neither.

IV.

Gentle MacNeice, excuse
Those misconceptions that
Once fell between us, those
(Like taking the wrong coat)
Errors that disclose
What is affectionate.
For God only knows
How hopeless our state
If it were not for those.

V.

And I would like to think
Whenever a pass or word
Comes clean and quick as a wink
That you have overheard
And elevate your drink;
For, to be absurd,
By such jokes, I think,
Your bones might be stirred.

VI.

And I remember you said
"All I have managed to learn"
And shook a fuzzy head
"Is not to mix grape and grain"
And at these words I heard
The sobersided turn
Away, and seek instead
Truths too big to discern.

VII.

Thus I would like to hope
The ironic Horatian
Ode that in its scope
Looks no larger than
A pocket telescope
Taught your verse to scan
The dying skies of Europe
With the eye of a man.

VIII.
So, trusting that you now
Hold the forgiving mood—
(I write this, anyhow
Most for my own good)
May the grass grow
Greener where your blood,
Irishman, goes to show
Others where you stood,
Others how to grow.

Rome

No Other Tiger Walked That Way That Night

No other tiger walked that way that night.
She tied her hand with promises to the gate,
She gave her head in red on a golden plate,
She hung her heart out on a begging arm:
No other tiger walked that way that night.

She wound her bowels out around a tree,
She shed astrologies of tears; she bled
Till the seas choked with love unsatisfied;
She nailed her sex with negatives to the bed:
No other tiger slept between her knees.

She stood on corners till the morning came
Mesmerising her misery with another day;
She wept in public; she died when a name
Was the same, or when a lovesong was over:
No other tiger came to be her lover.

She remembered the couch-kingdomed queens
Who keep their children inside contraceptives;
She tried to lead the simplest of possible lives;
Her room was always haunted by sweet dreams;
No other tiger spoke in superlatives.

No other tiger walked that way that night—
Not when she begged on the knees where
The sabre-toothed baby wrestled in its lair
Among her memories of an amorous May:
Not when she opened her future like a gate,
No other tiger ever entered there.
No other tiger, either by night or day,
Ever ever ever walked that way.

The Stabat Mater

The sorrowing mother was
standing beside the cross
    her son died on
as through her heart of hearts
pain like a flock of darts
    flew sobbing in.

O such affliction then
the mother of this son
    knew as she saw him,
she trembled where she stood
felt her own flesh and blood
    rush to adore him.

Who is the one will not
weep to see all that
    this woman suffers?
who without compassion
look on the immolation
    that she offers?

She saw her son rejected
her own son whipped and tortured
    for all men
she saw him hang in torment

till at the holy moment
    he lived again.

O fountainhead of sorrow
O mother teach me also
    to love as I mourn
tender me so much of
your sorrow and your love
    that my tears burn.

And, mother, grant that I
may seem also to die
    on my own cross
and let me also share
those wounds I cannot bear
    since they are his.

I gather my grief with
the tearglass of the truth
    and hope I may give
for that man crucified
tears not to be dried
    as long as I live.

Virgin of virgins, be
turned not away from me:
    grant I may bear
his death within me so
that I may also know
    how to die here.

O burning and burning by
you, virgin mother, I
    beg to be sheltered
when at the Day of Wrath
by that tremendous death
    everything's altered.

Virgin and queen of virgins
when that last day begins

O let me see
the dawn break on his face
and let his breath like peace
be borne upon me.

Grant me the shadowing
hand of his harrowing
nailed out on wood
and fortified underneath
the crucifix of his death
stand where you stood.

And when the flesh is dead
heaven from overhead
send down to me
out of the holy skies
the bird of paradise
from you to me.

On a Distant Prospect of English Poetry & Downing College

The waters we sit by
my dear, and weep
may not be very
wide or deep
but at least we
can see that the harp
is kept well strung
and the pencil sharp
for by this river
many sit
just staring down
into it
sighing because
they see the fish

can't be caught simply
with a wish.
And it's very hard
to land a verse
if your line's baited
with nothing worse
than abstract desire
or megapride
because the poem
like a bride
wants something solid
and upright
to get her teeth in
for a bite.
So fish with the dictionary
and your soul
on the intelligence
like a pole:
for the laws of English
Poetry
reduce themselves
to these three:
(you'll find 'em in
several versions
but all go back
to the Persians)
to speak the truth
and shoot straight
and make the mind
expiscate.

O the cultures are flocking
around the corpse
and Essays in Cretiny
gives a few yawps
as Dr. Prometheus
in his spectacles
speculates freely on
dialecticals
and the spirits of Downing

street or college
admit they's exhausted
human knowledge
so all that's left
for us to do
(never was so little
done by so few)
is simply to sit
on the ragged rocks
silently sighing
this paradox:
You downy birds,
desist, desist,
or you may find
you really exist.

What can we learn
from a loss so grievous?
Now we shall feel the
rigor leavis.
Abandoned? No,
the homonym
offends the lucid
mind of him
whom even the gods—
reduced to grammar
as inconclusive
as a stammer—
address in an
uncertain manner.
Farewell great doctor
of minor clauses
parentheses and
victorious causes
winged witticisms and
wingless horses.
How can we ever
really thank
a doctor for being
so very frank

that every time
the queen sickens
he simply mutters
What the Dickens
and to our
extreme abhorrence
reveals to us
King Charles' Head
belongs in fact to
D. H. Lawrence.

Now there is nothing
left to do
but sit around
listening to
the memory of
that nurse and doctor
damning us worse
than any proctor,
till, like a toilet,
the vacant silence
(which might be the mind of
Didy Rylands)
fills with a kind of
reptilian hiss and
once again
we know we listen
one and all
to an emission
so full of gall
it sounds like pissing
against a wall.

Farewell master of
Eliot
(I mean the lady
of course, not
that rival critic)
farewell master of
the mephitic,

master of crafty arts
and farewells,
but master of absolutely
nothing else,
we hang on your word.
It never tells.

Funeral Eulogy for Robert Colquhoun

i.
It was at four in the morning at work on his sketch of Death
He felt on his shoulder the tip of that twisting wraith
He had at last etched on the negative of his life.

As the Flying Scotsman to the landscapes of the Pennine Chain
Or the Flying Dutchman to all illusions of the Ocean
So was Colquhoun to those through whom his devotion drove him.

What we saw was a winged engine illuminated with flame
Or the skeletal hull loom through the fog of our time
As he dominated and dogged the heart marked X.

I shall know him again by the self-graven epitaph in his face
When, as he may, he chooses to revisit the place
That gave him, as haven, little more than a grave.

Tenderest of men in the morning before the ravening ghouls
Swept out of his holyrood conscience like lost souls,
In the evening we heard him howling in their chains.

All things were, to this man, a sort of structural
Crucifixion, like the god of the straining pectoral
Brought down to the flayed stoat nailed to a tree.

I saw him with a single stroke so knife the nerve
Of a drawn form that in its convulsion it gave
Off life like a sigh and hung suspended there.

Aware long before we were aware that he was best dead
He waved his bony hand in a hieroglyph that said:
'I cannot rest. I leave the rest to you.'

And now this beautiful head and powerful hand
Which, between them, had so ennobled us, send
From nowhere the same message as before

When he taught us from the cell and through the bar:
'All things have been destroyed and therefore are
True subjects for their rebirth in our love'.

ii.

By moonlight I see a stallion of Stubbs-Uccello
Gaunt, long-barrelled, yellow, lifting its head
Proudly out of a fallow bunch of thistle

Which is the Knoxian conception of Scottish
Responsibility. And now this proud man is dead.
This Highlander, this skinny Ayrman, this, yes, British

Mountaineer of spiritual violence,
This draftsman who was not so much a painter
As the graphologist of our dying conscience,

Elected to go home to cold Kilmarnock
And render those he left behind a mere remainder,
For what he wanted lay north of Cape Wrath and the rock.

In the ferocious exhibition bout he conducted
With himself both Jacob and Angel, we, the audience,
Had at last become superfluous. We were subtracted.

I have to believe that, having contested the issue
With his own issue, he now resumes it in regions
To which neither our love nor our grief shall ever have ingress.

Intensity of spirit, that energy with which
Energy creates itself, is indestructible.
Now where is this wrestler Jacob meeting his match?

And, supernaturally, why? To that rigorous
Calvinist of the Image, canvassing the invisible
Icon in colours seemed at heart futile and frivolous.

What, I think, broke this horsebreaker of a man
Was the knowledge that not in things but in their distances—
Yes, there the love that kills them always began.

Such a hero—and by this I mean
A heart that acknowledges the glory of consequences—
Foresees that the love that generates between

All things must in its own turn destroy them,
Like rubbing hands of wood. What possible pretences
Existed for such a man? How could he employ them

In the theatre already burning of his spirit?
The consolation that pacifies those ashes
Is his. It is not ours. We cannot share it.

So let him lie now near the rock and the cold loch
Not to awaken again till Cape Wrath one day dashes
The last wave over that long grave in Kilmarnock.

Inscribed to Robert MacBryde

The Valley of Ariccia

O valley of Ariccia
my sunrise and my sunset are
hung here by the double star

as in its burning cage the day
with Venus in its lion eye
lies down along the evening sky

or crowing day up from the calm
of each sleep sequestered farm
the cock shakes like a golden palm

and the Alban hills stand round
hammering with the golden sound
like a harp hid in the ground.

The peasant climbs the morning hill
through treadmills of mimosa till
he seems to labour standing still.

O lovely valley of mimosa
each of your gilded days bestows
a love that gathers all things closer

as the doves gather in every tree
that voices in your aviary
all the devotion within me:

since like a cradle of the mind
here I and anyone can find
the love that nurses its own kind

for those lucky few whose birth
praised and is praised by this earth
know what such a love is worth.

Epitaph: On the Suicide of the Painter John Minton

Rest, Johnny, rest, rest,
Under your starry dirt;
The lifelong daymare's past.
Clawing those harpies tear
And rend your haunted heart
But you are not there
For at the lonely last
That hooked nail in the nerve
And the crisscrossrow bone
Know that you are gone.
And now that your Now is Never
At last, at last,
The three foul Furies must
Leave you alone for ever
Leave you alone, at last.

Formal Elegy on the Death of Oscar Williams

I

There by the stone in the short grass where, resting, you wait
with your spectacled eye turned on the road up which I approach you,
yes, I and all of us, sulking or shouting, some without gifts, and none
late,
and a few in the knowledge that if they should ever reach you
you will not, perhaps, be there, sad man of ashes, but gone
still further on seeking your republic of the elect:
and some come sober with excesses and some, not happy alone,
in processions of orgy like that Bacchanalian sect
who, cock-eyed and tiger-skinned dancing out of India, ride
astride their own backs to the grave; and some as to their home
walk truly up to the hot gate unhesitant, open-eyed,
unhelped by the three old hags—ah, wait there for a little time
by your stone, Oscar, and we shall meet as on many a former time.

II

Are the wraiths out there in the gardens where no summer storm
shakes them and no grief ever falls? Are those zany insomniacs there
the unAmerican nightingales, and do they perform
nightly for you as never, you said, they did here?
And the mad sun you once saw like Jehovah's head in the sky
aflame with rage, and prophetic with menaces,
burns it now there beside you, weeping from a crimson-lake eye
the pity you saw only in it and in no other face,
and was it, Oscar, your pity you saw in its face?

III

The dead are not dead as the stars or ideas die
so that nothing is left but ashes on time or the tongue;
their absences move about us like invisible eagles that fly
only just overhead so that we walk among
the benevolent empires of their jurisdiction, and even
when we are lost in the winter of Teuterberger,
these eagles are not lost. To each of us is given
the two-headed eagle of a dead friend as augur,
and for us these eagles weep in the crystal of winter.

IV

How can I mourn, my dear friend, when I think of you strolling
those high laurel-hung terraces your heart had so hankered for
as you perched like a parrot up in your cage by Bowling
Green? And only the ghost of a dead wife to open the locked door
of your loneliness and lead you among us? I cannot mourn
when I think of that meeting at last with her whom so long
you hung around here awaiting your too long delayed return
to, she that dead wife whose only commission of wrong
was that she died before you. So may, at your re-union,
the earth not separate you two again where you sleep
in the American grave, each with your long lost companion,
but may earth hold you both closer and together keep you.

Index of First Lines